D1564534

THE COLLECTED POEMS
OF WILBERT SNOW

The
COLLECTED POEMS
OF
Wilbert Snow

Wesleyan University Press

MIDDLETOWN, CONNECTICUT

This volume includes the poems originally embodied in the following books by Wilbert Snow: *Maine Coast,* Harcourt, Brace & Co., Inc., 1923; *The Inner Harbor,* Harcourt, Brace & Co., Inc., 1926; *Down East,* Gotham House, 1932; *Maine Tides,* Henry Holt & Company, 1940; and *Sonnets to Steve,* Exposition Press, 1957.

The poems "Fate of the *Royal Tar,*" "March Snowstorm," "November Interlude," "Return to New England" (originally titled "New England Return") and "Smelting" are copyright © 1936, 1940, 1941, 1940, and 1939 respectively by Yankee Inc. and are reprinted by permission from the pages of *Yankee.*

Library of Congress Catalog Card Number: 63-17797
Manufactured in the United States of America
First Edition

To Jeannette

Conflict

The sea is forever quivering,
The shore forever still;
And the boy who is born in a seacoast town
Is born with a dual will:
The sunburned rocks and beaches
Inveigle him to stay;
While every wave that breaches
Is a nudge to be up and away.

CONTENTS

SONNETS TO STEVE AND OTHER POEMS

MAINE COAST

The Paving Quarry

Our pathway led through birches shoulder-high;
'Twas autumn, and the little yellow leaves,
So slender were their stems, seemed poised in air,
And gaily did they flutter in the wind.
The huckleberry leaves shone brilliant red,
And bayberry scattered incense on our way,
As now we walked through plots of velvet moss,
And now on granite ledges gray and hard.
Abruptly came our journey to a stop,
And there in ragged grayness lay the quarry.

"This pavin' motion," my companion said,
"Was goin' to make me rich, and made me poor.
'Twas in the *'eighties* I began work here,
When all great cities paved their streets with blocks.
A nickel apiece they were, and I could reel
Two hundred blocks or more each blessed day.
The reelin' wa'n't much like the reelin' now:
'Most anything would do. Along this hump
Were fifty motions clickin' every day.
Beside that barrel there filled up with chips
I reeled, the happiest hours of my life,
I wouldn't say how many thousand blocks,
While Fred, my butty, plug-drilled and broke stone.
I somehow liked the music of the sound,
The click-clack-clickin' of a hundred drills
From all these motions in among the trees.
How different now, when all you ever hear
Is chickadees, or crickets, or the frogs!
I sometimes think they liked the noises, too,
Of hammers clickin', and the rattlin' wheels
Of wagons, or the creakin' of the hames
In horses' collars on these rocky roads.
For we were prosp'rous then; at half-past four
'Most any night but Friday you could smell
Beefsteak a-fryin' anywhere in town,
And hear the snap and sizzle in the spider.
(We can't afford to eat beefsteak today.)
'Twas fun at night to see the youngsters bolt

To meet their daddies, grab the dinner pail,
And find a cookie or a piece of cake
Left there like toll-bait to be sure they came.
'Twas fun just after supper to drop 'round
To Em'ry's store, and hear the boys run on.
They'd smoke, and fight John L.'s big mills again,
With Paddy Ryan, Mitchell, Jake Kilrain—
They never loved another like John L.
And sometimes, when the bottle went around,
The boys would sing. I wish you could'a'heard
Mike Flemin' sing 'The Wind that Blew Across
The Wild Moor'; somethin' in his Irish voice
Would make you think o' lonely winds at night,
And cryin' children strayin' on the moor.
And then on Saturdays we'd have a dance,
And start it with a breakdown in the store.
I always liked the breakdown best; the boys
Were keyed just right, the jew's-harp twanged and twanged,
The harmonica began with 'Home Sweet Home,'
And Cowin', wounded at Bull Run, would clog,
And dance the 'buck and wing' in perfect time.
Then all would leave to join the 'march and circle'
Except the old men who would set and smoke.
Ah, them were jolly days; I never thought
They'd leave us as they did; the price went down,
And cities paved with asphalt room o' blocks;
The young folks moved away, but we were old,
Too old to think of other towns as home—
And there we were without a place to farm,
Who might'a'had ten acres turned to field.
Perhaps it's just as well. A hundred hens,
A little garden truck, a chance to fish,
And time to talk of pranks we did as boys—
One way of life's as good's another, I guess,
If we just take it right—that's all that counts."

He gazed along the west; the golden sun
Was streaming through a clump of tall spruce trees.
The dead, low limbs, transfigured in the light,
Had brought the sunset near; the background stood
In lemon-colored glory; back we turned

4

Without a word, and down a birch-fringed path
We found the road that led our footsteps home.

George McGoon

I

Slim George McGoon on Sunday night
Had just one answer, "That's a' right,"

To every questioning of mine
When I was but a child of nine,

And he was on his weekly bout
With Scotch, his lotus flower for doubt.

He staggered from the barn or shed,
Whose stanchions flocked about his head,

Past cluttered pickaxes and hoes,
And other obstacles that rose

To make his progress one long maze
Of fresh adventures lost in haze.

My mother often took the key
And went away forgetting me

Out playing in his yard next door
Where pups rolled on the chickweed floor;

There tiredness waylaid my eyes,
Taking its toll of childhood cries,

Till he would come and hold me tight
In his rough arms, with, "That's a' right."

II

On weekdays with his dinner pail,
Or coming from the evening mail

In summer, twilight would intrude
His spirit's dusty solitude:

The beams would dance in yellow rays
And draw from George another phrase

Whose words, immeasurably slow,
Were, "I don't know; well, I don't know."

I've seen his eyes grow dappled gray
Upon a stirring stormy day;

Or when a neighbor had been laid
Away beneath the poplar shade,

And thoughts of soul-life after death
Were holding everybody's breath;

Down through the pasture woods he'd go
With, "I don't know; well, I don't know."

The mellow Sunday mood was best
For his thin vein of sharp unrest,

For all his choicest blessings then
Were lavished on the sons of men—

Relieving the agnostic mood
That tortured him in sober blood.

And thus his life, through shine and snow,
Was, "That's a' right," and "I don't know."

The Eagle

A hundred kingbirds flying near our ship
On Fundy's Bay becalmed, one glassy morning,
When white sails quivered and the reefpoints flapped,

Could not as much as stir the drowsy crew,
Swabbing down decks and parching in the sun,
To lift their eyes above the galley stovepipe
Till, from the north, a grim, bald-headed eagle
Swooped in among the flock exultingly,
Causing a flutter, as a great world figure
Bestirs an audience that has waited hours.
The kingbirds swarmed about and heckled him,
Setting us all blood-hot to take his part;
And when their heckling grew so violent
They clung to him as barnacles to rocks,
In ever widening circles up he soared
With scores of groundlings darting in his wake.
We watched them, baffled, drop off one by one;
Now twelve were left; now five; now only three;
And finally, with one victorious wheel,
He thrust his golden wings through the yielding blue,
Till heights divided his majestic being
From birds that never knew the upper air.

From spellbound admiration we tore loose
And cheered him as we would a racing yacht
Defeating rivals in a piping breeze.

I came back to my squeegee suddenly,
And never on this planet do I hope
To look upon a countenance transfigured
As was our mate's funereal, cidery face—
Our mate, a shattered mast, his warped hands trembling,
His mouth proclaiming cynic dissipation,
His slouchy clothes announcing him a failure;
Yet his brown eyes at times flashed smoldering fires,
And when he straightened up to give an order,
We felt behind him clean-cut generations,
And sensed a tithe of what he might have been.

"You wonder, Bill, what's running through my mind,"
He took my arm and led me toward the anchors,
"I'll tell you, Bill, I read the Bible once;
I read, and learned by heart a place which said

That 'they who waited on the Lord renewed
Their strength: they mounted up on wings
Like eagles; they would run and not be weary,
Would walk and not be faint.' The man who wrote
That text, Bill, must have seen a flight like this."

He stopped; and I respected what was in
His eyes enough to keep the silence with him,
While forces not of earth like giant tides
Of Fundy's Bay were flooding ugly flats
And dingy marshes of his low-drained life.

He left the ship at Montreal, and bore
The lighted countenance and eagle mood
When he shook hands good-by.
                                    I watched him lose
Himself among the crowds that filled the dock,
While fragrances of dusk were wafted inland,
And stars were coming out above the harbor:
A wounded eagle, game for one more flight,
He seemed a soul apart—his wistful face
Deep bronze and mystic, hauntingly detached,
The timid sailor just ashore, at strife
With that which wakened when he saw the ascent.
The thickening shadows wrapped him round about
As gently as the water wrapped our keel,
And big, dark rolling clouds shut out the stars
As evening met the coming on of night.

Crump Cook

When war broke out in 'seventeen
The Flanders' slaughterhouse had been

So deftly flashed on Western eyes
By propaganda's dark disguise,

That Crump decided not to go,
Likewise his buddy, lazy Joe.

But when they saw each buck in place
With clean brown suit and clean brown face,

And saw good dogs forsake the city
For barracks life austere and gritty;

And saw the lights that glittered through
Girls' eyes on Thursday's gay review;

And found themselves despised and lonely
With old rheumatic cripples only,

Their marching feet could not keep still
Till they joined the hunt for Kaiser Bill.

The draft-board patriots looked amazed
As on these two old bums they gazed;

A doctor, with a stethoscope,
Stepped out to scan these dregs of hope;

Forlornly muttered, "This way, boys,"
And like two convicts sick for noise,

They took ten steps and heard their doom
Pronounced by Science. Oh, the gloom

That weighed them down as they walked out
And felt the world sink round about

Their eyes as they moved off to impart
That one had hernia, one weak heart.

Could martyrs crucified or burned
Feel worse than these two hulks interned,

The day the company, banners wide,
Marched through the streets with splendid stride?

Folks sang such songs as "Over There"
Before the pastor offered prayer;

And just to add a New England touch,
Lest gaiety be stretched too much,

Some woman started "Shall we meet
Beyond the River," and the beat

Of that grave hymn revealed the mood
In Uncle Sam's crusading blood.

That afternoon the long main street
Took on a look more gray and neat;

Crump never felt such gloom before,
Madness assailed him more and more.

Till he resolved to drown his troubles
In Prohibition booze's bubbles.

They seize Crump's speedy motor craft,
Clean-lined and slim from fore to aft,

And chug-chug down to Barney's Inn,
A place unspeakable of sin,

With wine and women, but little song
To hold a true Bohemian long.

A pair of hardwood cellar stairs,
The gangplank of the *John F. Sayres,*

Led to the forecastle below,
And when their eyes began to grow

Accustomed to the light, they viewed
Five men, in various stages, stewed.

A veteran of the Civil War
With long white beard, stood up and swore

That Yanks could fight, by God, the best
Of all earth's soldiers, East or West.

10

A fat, good-natured, silent rummy
Rose from the corner like a dummy

Propelled by wires, and exclaimed
"Hurray!" and sank back unashamed.

As the war talk buzzed, our fading flowers
Felt meanly stung with the stinging hours,

For ten good shots had made them strong
Enough to lick the German throng

That bayonetted Belgian babies
And filled the wells with germs of rabies.

If Uncle Sam could turn them down,
They'd have revenge or wreck the town.

So clambering up the gangway scuttle
They tried a trick more grim than subtle.

The Stars and Stripes above the Inn
Waved softly and expressed chagrin,

Or so they thought, as Crump and Joe
Unloosed the halyards and hauled low

The flag, and quick as lightning's flash
Tied two rum bottles on the lash

And hoisted them to the flagpole's top
And cheered till they were like to drop.

The hundred-per-centers down below,
Alert to any brand of show

From a dogfight to a circus tent
Rushed up the gangplank, action bent.

They 'phoned the sheriff of Blue Ridge
To come and view this sacrilege;

And down he plunged, his ardor burning
While the two ran off, and quickly turning

The wheel, sped past lobster cars,
Wetting their rusty iron bars.

The sheriff saw them making off,
And though he knew the veteran's cough

Was in itself a hint that law
Was not exactly held in awe

At Barney's grim, secluded place,
He winked at this, but blazed in the face

To see those two rum bottles hung
Where the Stars and Stripes had proudly flung.

The sheriff said, "I'll teach that scum
A lesson if you two will come,"

(He pointed to a sober pair
Of fishermen whose craft lay there)

"And let me have your lobster wherry
To catch them bastards. Let us hurry!"

The three sped south without delay
And flew across Penobscot Bay;

But nature had to spoil the fun,
Just as the contest had begun

A fog bank drifted in toward shore
And nothing but a distant oar

Within a rowlock, or a sound
Of motor chugging out around

Was left to guide the expectant crowd
Whose fervor now was deep and loud.

12

More zealous still were the racing crews;
They hardly knew what course to choose;

But Crump cared least, and let her slide
Down channel, gas valve open wide;

A glorious hour of chase had sped,
When two big breakers loomed ahead;

And soon more breakers in commotion
White-crested on the dark green ocean

Sent fear along Crump's trembling breast,
And made Joe's teeth seethe like the crest

On top the wave just after breaking;
They wondered what cove they were making

If cove at all, and Joe shouts, "Pull
The switch off, Crump, or we'll swamp full."

Crump pulled the switch, and listening
Could hear a bell buoy's ding-dong-ding;

Could hear tugs shrieking up the bay,
Their sirens warning, "Clear the way";

Could hear the noisy tuck-tuck-tuck
Of gasoline boats out of luck;

Could hear the breakers all about them
Roll up and break, enough to rout them,

If one should break beneath their bow;
And Joe said, "Crump, where are we now?"

Said Crump, "I'll tell you where we are;
I hear the rote on Sheepscot Bar;

I'd know it if it broke in hell,
I've heard it break for such a spell

Jigging out round here hauling pots."
Just then it broke in hell; green knots

Of water heaped themselves together
On the starboard side like a great bellwether,

And growing horns of widening white
Came tearing through with plunging might

And butted mercilessly down
Their craft and left them there to drown.

The ice-cold water chilled their knees
And backs till they were like to freeze;

But both could swim, and out they struck
Relying on the Lord and luck.

A big wave caught them in its hand
And washed them on the rocks and sand.

A flock of sandpeeps on the beach
Flew up and wheeled well out of reach;

Preened themselves and jerked their tails
Spread out their wings like new white sails,

And wondered who had come so rude
To wreck their ocean solitude.

Our heroes staggered up the shore
And flopped like two drowned rats; Joe swore

His knee and elbow both were breaking
With painful tingling, ceaseless aching.

A chill wind pierced their bodies through
Like a splitting knife; their hands turned blue;

Like groggy fighters up they crawled,
Found them a cave securely walled

And went to sleep. The sheriff's packet
In blind pursuit slowed down its racket

And steered a far more cautious track
Among the buoys red and black;

They shut their engine off and strained
Their ears, so sensitively trained

By custom, they could quickly tell
Crump's engine from the rest, and fell

To wondering why its chug-chug-chug
Had altogether ceased; they dug

A compass from the ditty box
And took their bearings from the rocks

They knew most accurately, when
The keener of the sheriff's men

Made out a speck of gray-blue flannel
Swift floating down the foggy channel;

They reached for it and found Crump's hat
And near at hand Joe's derby, flat.

A bailing scoop, a lobster measure
Confirmed the worst; at once their pleasure

Gave way to honest neighbor sorrow;
"The town will hate us all tomorrow,"

They thought, cursed deep their zeal and turned
Their wherry round and homeward churned.

The betting crew that lined the wharf
Looked once and knew all bets were off;

They hurried home and told their wives
Who mourned the loss of two gay lives

That gave the village half its lore
Of evening jokes at the grocery store.

"Well, Crump was not half bad," they said,
"He mended many a broken sled

For children, and repaired the toys
And smelt lines of a hundred boys;

And Joe got up a sawing bee
For Widow Barnes and her small three,

And made such fun, with all his fuss,
He'll be more missed than ten of us."

The pastor thought a service fitting
For these two men, and at one sitting

All hands said, "Yes," and three days later
The village church enclosed a greater

Array of folk than ever dressed
For Sunday service in their best.

Meanwhile our pair on Sheepscot Bar
Had sobered off; a lobster car

Had served them for a place to sleep;
They drank from fresh springs cool and deep;

They lived on berries red and blue
And watched to see the sun burst through

Its thick damp cover; those three days
Had made them vow to change their ways.

At ten the third long-lagging day
A sloop from the islands in the bay

Slid by and saw our Crusoe, Crump,
And his Man Friday on a stump,

And sent a towboat toward their station
To break their sober isolation.

Three hours more, they reached the town
And seeing carriages, swooped down

To church, determined to find out
What all the rumpus was about.

They poked their heads past a window sill
Just as a hymn closed; all was still.

The pastor said, "We know the sin
That lured our two late brothers in;

It was the demon rum, whose powers
Have wrecked so many a home of ours;

The German curse outraged their sense
Of decency and right, and hence

They burned with zeal to avenge the shame
Of bleeding Belgium in God's name.

They had their faults, as most men do,
But to the old flag they were true.

And I would wrap around Crump's shroud
Its folds of which we're all so proud."

Joe looked at Crump, Crump looked at Joe
And said, "I guess it's time to go,"

And through the pasture woods they slunk
To ride the rods of the fleet Grand Trunk,

That fire by night and cloud by day
For sons of Israel gone astray.

Mail Time

The full moon staggers from the quivering sea,
Turning to glistening white the snow-thatched roofs,
And silhouetting limbs of maple trees
Against the moon-white homes and big red barns
That catch the wind's moan in the dead of winter.
The crisp clear spirit of the night calls forth
Hallos that echo through bare pasture woods,
And stillness holds the flushed pearl-handled shoreline
Securely on the knife-blade of the tide.

Faint sleigh bells ring far up the winding roadway,
And speed the lagging pulse beat of the village.
The crunching snow beneath expectant feet,
The clear, sharp bells of neatly painted sleighs,
One with a lover and his smiling sweetheart—
The opening and closing of shed doors,
The dull, slow cowbell on a farmer's woodsled,
The steady click of oars in distant rowlocks,
Proclaim to everyone, "The mail has come!"
And in the post office the people gather
So thickly that the carrier with mailbags—
A lame, grease-spotted, walrus-whiskered veteran—
Must wriggle like a skilful football player
To break his way through groups of waiting neighbors.

Before the numbered boxes in the corner
The little girls, in faded woolen dresses
And tightly braided pigtails tied with twine,
On tiptoe stare excitedly for tidings
Of brothers overseas or out West ranching,
Or brothers office-bound in busy cities.
The bigger girls distribute knowing glances
From eyes that flash the code of silent comment,
Whenever Frone, the postmistress, stops pounding
Ker-stamp, ker-stamp, ker-stamp, on fifty letters,
And takes time out to read a scrawling postal.

The old men in a circle round the fire
Dig out and fill their pipes as they spoon out

And tamp a lewis hole in ash-gray quarries,
Converse about the weather and deplore
The backing of the wind, and prophesy
A heavy snowstorm, if the changing moon
Does not bestir herself to stave it off.
The three survivors of the Civil War—
Stout Eben, with his right forefinger curled
Around his T. D. stem (he lifts it high
Whenever he removes it for a speech);
Old Tower, with his long, white, flowing beard
Just reaching to his lap when he leans forward
To praise the strategy of George McClellan;
And Jonathan, lean boyhood friend of Eben,
Nicknamed "By Joe," to fit his favorite oath—
Retell the dashing stories of Bull Run
And Fredericksburg: and Eben always mentions
The playing of the band across the river
That night at Fredericksburg: his hair stood up
To hear the band play "Dixie," and deep shame
Rushed over him that he should like it more
Than his, replying bravely with "John Brown."
The flutter of the youngsters at the mail
Perturbs these patriarchs little, for their day
Of getting letters vanished long ago
Beyond the woods of age, too bare of leaves
To catch the afterglow and bring it back.

"The mail is open," pipes the Ever Faithful,
And one by one, the bashful and the bold,
Alive with hope, confront the small square window.
The village belle takes up a clean white letter
And smiles her swift way out, while others watch her.
The frozen earth, to her, becomes a carpet
Of gorgeous tapestry on which she floats
Through some dim Oriental crystal palace,
Where hidden orchestras near marble fountains
Play bits like "Silver Threads Among the Gold."

A shy-faced boy, with mystical detachment
Apparent in his eyes and on his mouth,
With dreamy otherworldness in his walk,

And head just slightly tilted to one side,
Takes tremblingly his twice rejected poem
That vaguely phrases dim, aspiring visions.

The drawn, pale man, with stonecutter's consumption,
Recoils with fear to see a lawyer's letter,
And slinks away without a word of greeting.

The cocksure dude, expecting special matter,
Rejects the shaking of Aunt Fronie's head,
Insisting he has something in the mail,
At which an altercation soon brings out
Aunt Fronie's rapier gift of shining speech
Whose cutting epithets thrust in and twist,
Driving the youth for refuge to the sidewalk.

The village wag sends home a bunch of postals
From Boston to his friends: "Wish you was here."
"Played checkers with the Iron Man last night
At Austin Stone's Museum. Did he beat me?
Well I should say so; take him on yourself once."
"Having a swell time. Went out to Harvard College,
And seen the flowers at the Agassiz,
They beat the posies in Aunt Cal's front yard."

The crowd thins out. The old men take their papers
And face again the clear December night.
A slamming door far down the village street
Tells loudly someone's disappointed heart.
The merrily jingling bells of sleighs that carry
Well-wrapped-up lovers, ring melodious mockery
To Jeremiahs preaching staves of doom.
The dull, slow cowbell on the farmer's woodsled
Tells neither joy nor sorrow, for the men
Who ride it have turned in the quiet wood road
Leading along earth's still, gray, neutral slopes.
I listen for the oars in distant rowlocks,
And only hear the far-off moaning rote
Of ocean on the ledges in the harbor.
At nine the village lights are out, and all

The beauty of the town beneath the stars
Is wrapped once more in silence as the last
Faint tinkle of the mail team dies away.

Olaf

From Sweden forty years ago he came
And settled in our village on the coast,
Casting his lot as one of us—a man
Who loved the sea as those alone can love her
Whose childhood longings have been stirred to life
In words made music by her mighty voice.

I never knew a man who loved the sea
As Olaf loved her; forenoons out of mind
In boyhood days have I beheld him loaf
The morning through, beside a shelving rock
In a little yellow dory, his right hand
Aclasp two eight-foot oars, a black clay pipe
Between his teeth; loaf long and long, and watch
The dark brown rockweed rise and fall, and rise,
With motion not quite regular; watch, too,
The smoky-colored periwinkles cling,
Or zigzag through the green two fathoms down
And nestle on the bottom strewn with kelp
And soggy wood and starfish pink and white;
Or take a listening mood and hold his breath
To hear the barnacles along the rocks
Disturb the silence of that quiet cove
With little seething, whispering monotones
That are, to stormy poundings of the bay,
As chirrupings of songbirds in the trees
To midnight forests crashing loud with storm.
I heeded in his steady eyes of gray
A glassy token which the old gray mother,
To mark him for her own, had spread about
His seaward-gazing countenance—a look
Found nowhere but in men who breast strong tides.

He seemed as much a part of that small cove
As did the crying sea gulls on the bar.
He drifted at the ebbing of each tide
Out over eelgrass to his cherished weir
Between the island and the harbor's mouth,
And climbed the stakes to look for schools of herring.

For twenty years expectantly he pulled
His wherry to the weir and back again;
For twenty years he thought about the tides
And dreamed about the mystery of skies;
And sunsets played around his wrinkled cheeks
And lit them as they lit the rolling calm
Of waters stretching out to evening sea.

His first score years with us he was content
To tend his lobster pots; but when he saw
His neighbors building weirs and growing rich
(A man who saves ten thousand we call rich)
He plunged with high adventure like the others,
Sold out his traps, and launched his life anew.
He paid a ragged group of men, and worked
On pocket, pound, and leader, day and night,
Spending a harvest garnered through the years,
Borne up by dream-propped, cedar stakes of hope.

Strong tides flowed in as only tides of spring
In that bleak northern land can flow: they rise
Full sixteen feet above low-water mark,
Flood the wharfs, and loosen old dried rockweed,
Stuck through with sticks, tossed up a year before.
They set adrift old fishing barrels, tarred
To keep them watertight, and slabs of spruce
Thrown up by woman's hand for winter's fire;
And when all these come drifting with the tide
At twelve o'clock, their weird and motley shapes
So variegate the surface of the bight
That one imagines gorgeous treasure chests
Afloat from some old pirate ship of Spain,
Or fabulous ambergris, near which there lurks
A sea serpent cavorting on the waters,

And scores of other wonders dotted round
The sun-bedazzled surface of the sea.

But these tides came and went with never a catch
For Olaf in his fortune-tempting weir.
Other spring tides swept by, and, year by year,
They brought him only deeper poverty.

At times he wished he never had forgone
The steady work of lobstering, and plunged
The savings of his youth adventurously;
At times he vowed he never would rebuild
The weir another spring.
                              Then spring would come,
And with it come new hopes and new desires.
And ever in recesses of his mind,
Reopened by the fragrances of spring,
He saw a thousand shining bushels swim,
And show their cool green backs in darting schools,
Huge smacks impatient for the ebbing tide,
And seining time an hour of pure delight,
With herring boiling in the pound so thick
The purse strings could not be drawn tight beneath
Until a dory load or two were dipped
To keep the bulging twine from bursting through.

With this he drove new stakes and cut new brush,
Repaired the breaches winter ice had made,
Stretched out his leaders to the harbor's mouth,
Put twine around his pocket, tarred his seine;
And as he smelled the pungent, boiling tar,
He dreamed his April dreams of wealth and ease.
He smiled upon his work indulgently,
For what is lovelier than a herring weir?
Two magic circles touched by two long lines,
Harmonious lines, and glimmering colored lights
Amid the silver grays of high-tide rocks,
And breasts dark brown of island shores laid bare,
Whose fluttering pulses call the evening star
To hasten from southeastern corridors,
And crown its rounded grace with one more charm.

But spring would pass, and long bright summer days
With southwest breezes every afternoon
For weeks together follow; yet, to him
The tides brought only added store of dream.

And so he lingers in his little skiff
While each succeeding moon beguiles the tides,
Scanning each change the setting sun displays
As it glides down behind the darkening trees,
To tint his herring weir with promised gold.

Fog Battalions

The big battalions of the fog whose dark
Gray horses kick up clouds of dust, roll in
And shut from sight the amber-dazzling sea.

The lighthouse men, with peering, sharp sea faces,
Start up the boiler in the whistle house
And bell-house two miles farther up the bay,
And soon the deafening blasts and deep-toned bells
Begin to fire at the oncoming host,
Exploding loudly, booming dismally
In fierce bombardment through the long, dark night—
Enough, my boy's heart felt, to scare the fog
Into an unstrategic, wild retreat.

How frightened as a child I stopped my ears
Before that screeching, unrelenting whistle,
And pictured it as some huge beast in pain!
How many times I stood upon the headland
Beside the lighthouse of my island home
And watched a schooner blossom from the fog
Arrestingly as flowers halt a man
Who, for the first time after dreary months,
Beholds them pushing from a bed of snow
In some Alaskan valley late in May!
How many hours have I watched the fog
Sway in and out with rhythmic rise and fall

Before receding to translucent calm!
For fog, too, has its seasons, like the winds,
The tides, and flowers, and months, and evening stars!
It weaves impressionistic colors on
The canvas of the air, till every cove,
And bay, and bight is wholly blotted out;
Then silently it traipses up the shore,
And inland for the space of half a mile
Spreads over hayfields and low alder swamps,
Hanging small pearls on spruce limbs, ferns, and grasses;
And when it has obscured the sea and sky
So hopelessly that noonday turns to dusk,
It stands, like a dissatisfied creator,
And rubs again the canvas of the air,
Letting the sunlight play on it once more,
And letting joy play upon the boatman's eyes
That could not see ten yards before his bow,
And feared a crash while fumbling through the mist.

Cyrus

The evening Asbury died I went to watch
Beside his coffin through the long, still night,
A mellow winter's night of melting snow,
And as I neared the house I felt the spell
That always filled our village when the dead
Were lingering among us in deep silence.
I turned the doorknob softly and stepped in
To find the table spread, the coffee pot
Beside the stovepipe on the kitchen stove,
Bubbling and spurting forth a steamy fragrance.
The parlor hanging lamp, not often lit,
Shed ruddy light against the household gloom.

Three neighbors greeted me in friendly tones:
The first one, Tom McKellar, village blacksmith,
Who read the Bible constantly and loved
To argue on its mysteries with the doctor
And other unbelievers in the town;

The second, Adam Kirk, a lanky Scot,
With mind as free as Tom's was Bible-bound,
Who broke each Sabbath tramping with a gun
Through deep spruce woods, or fished by smelting brooks,
His relaxations from another week
Of chipping ashlar in the barren stonesheds.
The third and last among the watchers, Cyrus,
Of massive frame and calm, hypnotic face,
With dappled freckles in his big gray eyes,
Stretched out full length upon a haircloth sofa
To ease the pain a wooden leg was kindling.
His voice held overtones from out-of-doors
Which stirred in me desire to learn the secret
That made him such a stout New England oak.

Without a sentence, Cyrus took the lamp
And led us to the damp, chill sitting room
Across whose corner Asbury lay at peace
In a long black casket trimmed with silver handles.
An evening wind just stirring as we entered
Swayed the white curtains of a lifted window,
Making a ghostly awe come down upon us
That hushed our voices to a reverent whisper.
We looked in every hour until twelve,
And passed the interim in random talk,
Now calling up details of Asbury's life,
Now mulling over gossip in the village.
From time to time a neighbor ventured in
To volunteer his service as a watch,
But finding four of us already there,
Would put his lantern down, stay long enough
To light his pipe, then say "Good night" and leave us.

At twelve we sat around the kitchen table
And talked until the barriers of day
Were down, and man to man we found ourselves
Strolling into each other's pastures, lingering
In genuine communion such as happens
But once or twice in any human lifetime.
The talk quite simply turned to unseen forces
Beyond the world of matter, Tom protesting

That simple Bible faith was all sufficient
To forge man's metal for the flint of death.
The Scot reiterated his release
From creeds and dogma, praised Bob Ingersoll,
And pooh-poohed tales of Spiritland as traps
Designed to frighten children, catch old women,
And snare red-blooded workmen up like rabbits.

Expectantly we turned to look at Cyrus.
He took his wooden leg off, placed it under
The lounge, where it would not be gazing at us,
And hesitated long before he spoke.

"I used to think as you do, Adam, once,
But since this leg was shot off I feel different.
And now I'll tell you things I almost never
Say a word about. The night before
My accident we all were going gunning:
A raft of birds was feeding round The Stallion,
And Two Bush Reef and Condor Ledge were black
With scads of coots; and low tide served at sunrise.
I reeved my tollers, cleaned my shooting iron,
And went to bed round nine o'clock, I guess.
At midnight I woke up and all was silent.
Till father's clock, that hadn't struck for years,
Up and struck one as plain as I am speaking.
I soon dozed off to sleep and had a nightmare,
Dreaming the air was full of little shot,
Bird shot, number eight or nine, I reckon,
And I was breathing them in throat and lungs;
They tore my chest and racked me all to pieces,
Till I woke up a lump of foggy sweat,
Resolving then and there I wouldn't go
To hunt for coots no matter what the day was.

"I woke up Emily and told what happened,
And she allowed that I had had a warning
And shouldn't go. Next morning bright and early
The boys come over yelling, 'Wake up, Cyrus!'
And I went down and told them I wa'n't going.
They asked the reason why. I wouldn't answer.

They teased and plagued me till I up and told them.
They all yelled 'Booger-man!' and 'Superstitious!'
Till I was plumb ashamed, went back upstairs,
Hauled on my pants and said, 'Don't make a touse, boys,
And I'll be with you,' for that very minute
I'd 'ave faced the Devil himself and never flinched.

"It was a dandy morning to go gunning,
The grass was brittle and the meadow frozen
With thin shell ice that covered all the puddles;
And when the sun rose up I thought how silly
I was to give away to dreams and warnings;
But I had not been in the boat an hour
Before I saw a loon come up ahead
Not fifty yards; I reached and grabbed the muzzle
Of my old Parker laying there half-cocked
And pulled her toward me. Something caught the hammer
And off she went, my leg and half the gunnel
Of my brand-new dory blowed to smithereens;
And from that day to this when I've had warnings,
Without a word I've just obeyed their whispers.

"The night the *Portland* went down I was going
To row to Big Green Island; ducks and drakes
Had struck in round the ledges by the thousands.
(This leg off didn't cure me none of hunting;
I'm old, but when I hear the rabbit hounds
Go yelping through the alders in December,
They make what my ear calls a sweeter music
Than all the opera from here to Paris;
And old-squaws' *ah-ah-link* around the kelp rocks
Do more than rabbit hounds to get my blood up.)
As I was saying, when the *Portland* went down,
The calmest afternoon I ever saw,
A voice behind me spoke up, 'Don't go, Cyrus.'
I looked around for I was stacking tollers
In the stern of my big wherry; not a sound
Except the wash of waves along the beach,
And not a soul in sight could I see stirring.
I didn't feel right, walked up Jackson's field,
And moseying along through cat-o'-nine-tails

Beside the old deserted paving motion
I heard that voice behind me, 'Don't go, Cyrus,'
So I hauled up my boat.

                          A big northeaster,
The biggest here for more than sixty winters,
Came down that night and blowed great guns till morning.
From my back door next day I looked and saw
Five shipwrecks in plain sight, and one of them,
A lumber Johnny, had four strapping men
Stiff frozen in the rigging when we reached her.
Two hundred people went down on the *Portland*
And not a soul was left to tell the tale.
When I went over to the Head next morning
Dead birds were piled in windrows by the lighthouse.
I tell you ropes and anchors counted little
When that storm got rampaging down the coast;
If it had struck me in my lobster boat
I wouldn't be here now, and you all know it.

"At least I know that many spirits live
And circulate among us at odd times;
I don't know why they come; perhaps they are
The bashful ones who hate to leave the earth
Like folks we know that never leave the town
Where they were born—and I incline to that;
They tended children when we went away,
And now I think they're taking care of us."

He roused himself as if he had forgot
To do his duty by the darkened room,
Put on his wooden leg in solemn silence,
Apologized for talking of himself,
Knocked out the ashes from his pipe and took
Again the lamp and led us to the chamber.
By this time family footsteps overhead
And sunbeams playing on the silver handles
Of the coffin brought us back from that dim world
The speech of Cyrus had us living in.

The Return

His wanderings in Western states were wide:
He knew the velvet greens of Oregon,
The deep rich blues of Crater and Tahoe,
The splendor of the Rocky Mountain peaks,
The sunburned Arizona mesas stretched
In far-flung, weird, fantastic pageantry;
The fragrance of the desert sage at dawn,
The blood-red sunsets on the Great Salt Lake—
He knew and loved them all. And yet the soil,
The harsh New England soil was calling him,
And would not give him peace till he resolved
To write the old folks he was coming back.

A dreary week across the continent,
With sooty cars and jangling engine shrieks,
Monotony of cornfields, and delays,
Then four glad miles between him and his home.

October's winelike air caressed his cheek,
Wine-colored leaves clung to the maple trees,
And out across the east the sun came up
And turned to wine the pearl-gray wastes of sea.

Each turn of road brought back a childhood scene:
Here stood a dam his boyhood gang had built
To overflow a field for winter skating;
And here, beneath a bent-down limb, he caught
A rabbit in a snare, and felt remorse
To see the blood upon the snow next morning;
And here they built two forts, and, choosing sides,
Played North and South through many a Saturday;
And here the hill where lady-slippers grew
For his delight through warm sweet days of spring,
(New England spring, a rush of ecstasy)
And for a childhood sweetheart whom he gave
These pink surprises like her soft pink face,
Telling her they were shoes of whippoorwills.

He turned the final corner of the road

And straight before him loomed the willow tree
And cottage, white and green, beyond its shadow.

He crossed the threshold, warped and worn, to greet
The kindliness within the eyes of her
Who filled his mother's place—his mother free
Ten years before from life's New England winter;
He thrilled to see his weather-beaten father,
Now gray and hardy, a New England oak,
Foursquare to life's bleak-beating northeast gales,
Nobility in every deep-lined seam
That scarred his face for sixty Spartan years.

With eager eyes he climbed the steep back stairs
To view the spot he always called his own,
The room whose walls, if they could speak, might tell
Of high resolves, and dreams, and voyages,
From wanting to grow up to be a sailor
To pioneering for a world set free,
But there he found the choking, musty smells
Far different from his Western expectations,
And, baffled, raised the little chamber window.

He roamed about the house from nook to nook,
And in his sister's empty room he saw
A big brown Teddy bear a chum and he
Had brought to make her Christmas joys complete
When they came home from college, sophomores.

The rooms that echoed laughter year by year,
That rang alive all day with romping din,
Alive all night with seven dreaming children,
Were now as empty as his empty heart.
A breezy Western traveller, he had come
Expecting Time, that culprit, to stand still,
Obedient to his stubborn wilfulness,
But this search found him on the traceless path,
The path that leads one to the dreams of youth:
Realities, he said, were foes of dreams,
Realities were cold, though robed in furs,
And dreams were warm, despite all poverty,

His hopes in coming back were vanity,
And all his dream prints reeked with choking dust.

Dejectedly he stumbled down the stairs,
And from the small verandah he could hear
The vigorous, far-off music of the sea.
'Twas not for nothing that majestic sound
Had thundered on his inner ear at birth,
Or been the tuning fork his ancestry
For countless generations had obeyed
To pitch their song of life to, when in need.
He caught the dauntless note its iron voice
Forever sings to lift the hearts of men
To face life's great defeat unfalteringly.
It lifted him from caverns of despair
As sunlight cheered him after musty rooms;
And with a heart as far from desolate
As ledges in the harbor from decay,
He watched a rolling wave break on the bar,
And turned to tell the old folks of the West.

Mike

I see him yet, as he stood there that day,
I but a boy of nine, he three score two—
I see him, dressed in brand-new heavy tweed
That made him look a stranger on the lawn,
Instead of my dear, playful, singing comrade.
I felt myself resent his new gray suit
And new brown cane, with silver top, that took
The place of maple, elm, or birch shillalahs
He was forever losing in the dooryard.
In pride and dignity he stood that morning:
His hair and beard as white as Arctic snow,
Arbutus-tinted skin, inquiring nose,
His left leg stiff, his left eye robbed of light,
A ticket back to Ireland firmly sewed
Inside his coat, and in his heart a cry
That he might stay with us and die in peace.

Old Mike had lived with us for fourteen years,
Till, when our last small sister came, he swore
He would no longer be beholden to us.
As eldest son he would go back and claim
His half-forgot, ancestral property;
And as he talked there rose before him prospects,
Mixed up with emerald memories of youth,
Of cows, and sheep, and green, well-ordered gardens
In which he heard the cuckoo and the blackbird
So sweetly that his tongue framed living pictures
Until the loafing neighbors gathered round him
Thrilled to the bone at his romancing powers.
An independence pitiful to see
Awakened in that battered derelict
One morning as he sailed the dusty road,
And stopped to tell his plans to other wrecks,
Declaring he would voyage once again
To Bally Brack, Killarney, County Kerry,
And live with sister Mary till he died.

A large, well-meaning, noisily breathing woman,
With gold-rimmed spectacles and olive skin,
Who clipped her words in crisp, emphatic manner,
Hearing Mike's story and capricious wish,
Went promptly out to raise an ample purse
And send the homeless pilgrim back to Ireland.
A paper she put out among the stonesheds
And round the quarries where they all knew Mike,
Soon brought the means to fit him for his journey.

The day now come, he half-refused to go.
The Black Ball liner he came over on
Twice twenty years before, had met with storms
And nearly foundered; children died like rats,
And sickness made the steerage one long nightmare.
The vision of return now meant to him
That rancid voyage over once again,
And gloomier than before, for youth's red blood
No longer spurred his hesitating body
And lifted hardship to adventurous heights.

Another fear preyed up and down the streets
And alleys of his mind—the gnawing dread
That drink would whisper, "Drown your woes, old man,
'Tis more than you can bear without my cheer."
He knew he could not brook the awful heartache
Of separation from us, knew his strength
Would crumple up beneath the chiseling teeth
Of that grim rat who never takes the count,
When men like Mike are battling with temptation.
With these forebodings in his heart, and tears
Making a delta of his Celtic face,
He stood beneath a silver maple tree
Which he had helped set out in our front yard
Just fourteen years before, and said good-by.

Impatiently, we waited for the letter
He promised us; he could not write himself,
But Mary had kept touch with us each year,
And well we knew her stamps and handwriting;
But two months passed before we heard a line,
In spite of my two letters crammed with news
Of cats, and dogs, and shinnying tricks, and children . . .
And then one night our mother read us this:

"My brother Michael came home crazy drunk,
And we two sisters scarce knew what to do.
He talked about his property in wild
Confusing speeches and so moithered us
We sent for the police; and when they learned
This poor old place would scarce bring a thraneen,
They sent him to the workhouse. There he is,
And we go up to see him every week.
He talks about the children all the time,
Especially the lad that wrote us twice;
And now he's whittling something grand for him,
He says he'll send by post at Christmas time.
He takes on hard, and rues the unlucky day
He left the States, and curses bitterly
The lady who made up the twenty pounds,
Till I stop up my ears and pray God's Mother
Forgive him for the awful state he's in . . . "

34

A few months later came another note
From Mary telling us of one more voyage,
And this the last, that poor old Mike had taken.
"He seemed," the letter ran, "to be all right
In body, and the film that closed his eye
Had dropped away, and he could see like new.
But homesickness was always preying on him;
Poor man, he could not read to pass the time,
And did not pay much mind to these new faces,
But called for Tim, and Dan, and other men
I never heard of, and your seven children.
He seemed to love them all, but most the lad
That wrote us letters in a fine, bold hand.
And I am posting this new top he made
Himself to send, he said the lad would love it.
I saw him just three days before he died,
And he appeared, I thought, unnatural bright.
He said the night before a big banshee
Had put his paws upon the bedroom window
And gazed with steady eyes for hours at him,
Making him feel his end was very near;
And would I send the Soggarth up at once
To say the blessed mass; of course, I did;
There's nothing more, except he wailed and wailed
That he came over, and he looked so sad
And called so loudly for the lad he loved
That I fell into keening there with him,
Until a keeper told me whist my noise,
And I went home. Come Tuesday, Michael died,
God rest his soul, . . . "

A Lobster Catcher

At birth he heard the dauntless, sounding sea;
And when his eyes first left his mother's breast
And ventured to look through the cottage window,
He heyed aloud to see the tumbling foam,
And white gulls skimming out among the ledges.

As soon as he could walk he played around
Old fishing barrels on the beach, and ran
To help his father haul the wherry up,
Or toy with tangled rope and potheads thrown
In heaps beside the fish house. How he loved
The pungency of tar, the smell of laths,
The fragrant pitch of spruce boughs bundled up
For arching pot-limbs! How he loved the sand
That filtered in between his toes, ticklish
And warm beneath the glaring sun! The blue
And dainty pearl of sand-swept mussel shells,
The egglike smoothness of round popple stones
Rolling and rattling up and down the beach,
The wild sweet peas that bordered headland rocks,
Instilled in him the mood that shaped his mind
And made him what he was—a wistful, shy,
Tide-swept, and salty nursling of the sea.

At ten he craved to swim and scamper out
With other boys before the tide had wound
Its sinuous way over the shining flats.
Together they would strip and race about
In soft blue mud, beset with honey pots,
That spattered over their burning backs and arms,
And seek amid the eelgrass for the holes
Where lobsters came to shed in late July.
The tide rushed tousling in; they dived and swam,
And raced along the beach like savages,
Filling the woods with pagan shouts of joy
Until the ebb tide chilled the shallow cove,
And chilled their rigid faces blue as whetstones.

When maple leaves defied the year's old age
By dressing up in glorious crimson gowns,
He hunted hooks and sinkers in the barn,
Cut slender smelt poles, dug for angleworms,
And found a small grape basket in the cellar
To hold his catch.
                    With two unfailing pals
He took his muddy stand at half flood tide
Where branches leaned far out above the cove,

36

And waited patiently the telltale nibbles.
A cork goes sidelong out, then under water,
One of them lifts his pole up, bringing in
A sun-containing, wriggling, savory smelt.
The unaccustomed silence of the boys,
The quiet upward flowing of the tide,
Now broken only by the dying flop
Of fish within the basket struggling free,
Imbued his smelting hours with a tone
As mellow as a tanager's soft flight,
That never roughened till the lines were wound,
And, gaily chattering, all ran up to spread
Their various catches proudly out before
Unquiet mothers waiting their return.

At fifteen years he bought his first small boat,
And rigged her up with leg-o'-mutton sail
And centerboard to beat against the wind.
Over the dancing waves he spanked along,
Singing rough chanteys to the singing breeze
Whose bracing, salty flavor tanned his face
A shade as brown as cliffs along the coast.
A schoolgirl dancing gleefully about
Upon the wharf beheld his dancing eyes,
And wove a net of joy around his heart
That wrapped him as a fine-mesh seine enwraps
A school of herring when the purse strings pinch.
With her his herring net of happiness
Was full to overflowing; and, as bloaters
Leap and sparkle brightly in the sunlight
Sending a thrill among the eager fishermen
Whenever a seine is bulging in the weir,
So this youth-brimming pair flamed shafts of light
From eyes unjaded, when the yellow dory
Of love had windingly transported them
Within the tree-calmed, rock-walled, magic bights
Whose surface holds the deep blue of the sky,
And turns to gold and lapis lazuli
When sunset's orange blossoms filter through.

At twenty, locked in happy marriage ties,

They built a cottage on a rocky point
Not more than fifty feet from full high tide.
She went with him on summer afternoons
To read *East Lynne* or *Dora Thorne,* or talk
Of homely nothings while he set his traps
To catch the cunners for his lobster pots.
The "ghunk hole" where they fished was shelved about
On three sides with high cliffs and ocean bowlders—
Great savage women standing in the sea
Around whose loins the rockweed draped itself
Like skirts of hula girls in Honolulu.
The fourth side opened toward the western sea,
And round it at low water shining kelps
Came out like flowing-purple pansy beds
Upon the grape-bloom surface just as dusk
And shadowy cliffs began their rendezvous.

Industriously he hauled his lobster pots;
And dawn was sure to find him every day
Out jigging round or pulling at his warps,
Or squinting toward the toggles in the sunlight,
Whose every trap contained a gambler's chance.
What joy was in his eyes these morning hours
When four or five count lobsters bronze or black
Were clinging to the pot heads or the laths,
As he broke out a trap across the stern!
What blessedness was his when wearied out
By struggles with the tide and heavy hauling
He came ashore and felt the spindrift touch
Of her whose life gave lightness to his own;
Whose smile could compensate for small returns
Of dreary days, or toll of raging storms
That passed him not whenever northeast gales
Pranced up the coast, stirring the undertow
To launch its heavy gales against the cliffs,
In never-ending roar of deafening salvos—
The artillery music of storm-bitten caves.

Another year their bud of happiness
Bewilderingly bloomed a miracle,
And as they gazed on his rose-petaled face,

And read love's meaning in his sea-blue eyes,
They felt their natures wedded once again.
His gurgles, smiles, and yawns so filled their minds
That they would pinch themselves to make secure
They were not dwelling in a world of dream.
Out hauling on the bay the minutes flew
Like happy gulls, in spite of jellyfish
And gurry smarting on his sunburned arms,
Till he was back to see the boy again;
And when the baby's first white tooth came through,
He scraped a rusty pen and squared himself
To share the event with three far-distant friends
Who smiled at him as one gone madly drunk.
Two winsome years; then heaven smiled once more,
And brought these two another miracle,
A cuddling, smiling daughter who unclosed
From brother's heart the tendrils of her father's
And placed them firmly round her helpless own.

One daughter more, and four dirt-healthy boys
Arrived to weigh the drudging mother down,
And make her picture heaven in terms of rest.

At forty, with a troop of happy children
Exulting daily round his little cottage,
The father read the book of life anew.
His wife, child-conscious, merging every thought
In seven offspring, lived again in them
The smiles and tears of childhood, and, in dreams,
Would long to spend a Sunday afternoon
Upon the headland basking in the sun,
Enraptured in her husband's lusty arms;
While he dismissed all dream-romance like this
As silly folly, laughed her out of mood,
And puttering round the fish house, headed traps,
Rigged haddock trawls, or cleaned his twelve-gauge gun,
Preparing for the time when coots would dot
The bay, and send his sporting blood to mounting.

Here his romantic youth came back again:
A late October chill swept up the bay,

And codfish slowly swam around the rocks
With questioning heads and ever-moving tails,
And dressed themselves the color of the kelps.
The gray coots followed, and, in big, black flocks,
Took feed around half-sunken iron ledges
That struggled through the ocean at half tide.

He picks a morning when the sea is still
And low tide tallying even with the sunrise.
The night before he patches tollers' heads,
Makes ready boats and guns, and scans the weather.
His grown sons go to bed with all clothes on
For fear the early morn will find them napping.
They startle at the creaking of a door,
Or dead leaf blown against the window pane;
And when they smell the coffee down below,
Leap out of bed and clamber down the stairs,
And, in high spirits, rouse a white ash breeze
That speeds their boat toward ledges lying calm
As whales or blackfish on the dark gray tide.
The tollers anchored twenty yards away,
They go ashore and pull the dory up
Within the crevice of a ledge, and crouch
Shivering, with eye and gun alert for action.
"Heads down," is whispered from the man to windward,
And twenty seconds later as the spray
Is kicked up by the web feet through the water,
Off go the guns and three gray birds collapse;
Cold faces glow, as coots and old-squaws fall
Beneath the banging guns inflamed with joy;
While out of the sea the salmon-tinted sun
Illuminates the clinging periwinkles
To match the kindled faces of the men.

At sixty his old double-barreled gun
Lay rusting in the corner, for the boys
No longer coaxed him out across the bay.
His sons were grown to manhood: one, a dreamer,
Took lessons of an artist, and became
A landscape painter, worshiping his art,
Returning every summer to recapture

40

The color in the islands and the waves.
Another went away and won his place
Among the engineers of Michigan,
Came back for brief vacations, and displayed
A never-ceasing restlessness beside
The wharfs and fish houses along the beach,
And wished the languorous, loafing mood of youth
Might once again be his, but wished in vain.
The other five remained at home, or moved
To nearby towns, and lived the cycle over
Of village joys and sorrows, births and deaths,
Their parents knew for sixty seasoned years.

The mother saw her children's children come,
And felt the flowerlike bliss of motherhood
Flow through her aged arteries again;
She dressed more neatly, smiled benignantly,
Beamed in the presence of her strapping boys,
And blushed to hear her husband's tongue wag free
Of love to her long after love's repose.

At seventy his wet, neglected youth
Began to tell upon his brittle limbs.
He wore brass rings around his wrists to ward
Away rheumatic twinges, but the chains
Of age restrained him like a great sheet anchor.
He puttered round the fish house, telling over
The days of wrecks, wild storms, and mackerel schools
That plugged the coves and rotted on the flats;
Found fault with newer ways of younger men,
And felt the beauty of the northeast storms,
The beauty of the spruce trees mirrored in
The cove at sunset when no ripple stirred,
As he had felt them fifty years before.

One bright May morning spring seduced him off
To dig a peck of clams and steal away
Before the others of the house were up,
To handline cod far out on Long Point Shoal.
The wind blew on, he drifted out to sea
Till he was lost to sight beyond the bay.

The coast guard breasted combers mountains high,
But all in vain, for no one learned his fate.
His wherry drifted on a sandy beach
Full twenty miles away—his barvel, pipe,
And half-shucked peck of clams were found intact
Among the oars, and gaffs, and fishing lines;
But not a trace of what had taken him
Was ever wheedled from the witching sea.

Night after night his wife kept supper hot,
And stood at sunset many and many an evening,
A grandchild in her arms, and gazed and gazed
Out toward the eastern headland hopefully,
To see his wherry coming round the point.
Reluctantly the children led her in
Out of the chill of evening, but the light
That shone from out her eyes and on her face
Persuaded them she caught a passing glimpse
Of his familiar features in the twilight.
She stayed with them from May till early fall,
And when the maple leaves flared winelike crimson,
She rested from her watching, and reached out
Her hand to greet her mate of three score ten,
And mix her dust with earth, as his was mixed
With kelps and seaweed of the cleansing sea.

Country Funeral

The mother, lying on a couch, brought down
By loving hands from chill, damp chamber rooms,
Breathes out her last faint breath; the men
Who watch try gently to convey, in speech
Whose tones supply the touch of sympathy
The Saxon phrases lack, the grim, stark truth
Of death, forever old, forever new.

Bewildered comes the aged father near
To verify the heavy news he hoped
Would never reach his ears; he calls her name

So piteously the neighbors turn away
And leave him for a minute all alone.
The children venture in: one, wailing loudly,
No longer tries to hold her pent-up anguish;
Another calms himself, but cords that swell
Along his neck betray his grief no less.

A neighbor cautions, "Eben, don't you think
We ought to call an undertaker down?"
"Yes, David, will you see that Johnson comes?"

And David scans the weekly till he finds
The county undertaker's shapely card:
"In case of death call up the Funeral Home."

An hour later Johnson, robed in furs,
Steps softly in and grasps old Eben's hand
With firmer grasp than country people know,
Removes a black fur cap which hides a mat
Of flattened hair across a sloping brow,
And says, "Too bad, ... you had a lovely wife;
I'm sorry to be summoned down on this
Sad errand here tonight. I mourn with you,
And feel as if a dear one of my own
Had just gone out and left me sorrowful ...

"Of course, you'll not want anything that's cheap
For such a wife: the only thing for her
Is what we call a couch casket; you'll want
My motor hearse, and everything just right;
And I'll take special pains to come myself
To see that everything goes smooth and straight."

"But jest about how much will all this cost?"

"We'll not talk money matters here tonight;
I know your grief, and know that you will want
The very best of everything for her."

And Eben, groping feebly in the dark,
Takes Johnson's word and says, "All right, you make

The price as reasonable as you can make it.
I own my home, jest paid the last in June,
And that's as far as my poor ownings go.
I ain't had nary job of stiddy work
For 'most three years, my rheumatiz is bad.
But I will pay you anything you say
If you will only take into account
My circumstances and my feeble health,
And be as easy on me as you can."

The cottage funeral two days later draws
The villagers for many miles around.
For two sad days a vigil has been kept
Beside the coffin—old-time country custom;
For two days neighbors have brought cakes and pies
And other gifts of food—sincerest tokens,
Worth more than speeches, which they cannot make.
The village minister takes up his place
Beside the casket, and reads, deeply moved,
"Let not your heart be troubled, ye believe,"
And feels his faith acceptable to all
Who loved the wife, now pillowed beautifully
In marble-featured plenitude of death.
The nearest relatives, swathed deep in black,
Are seated in a row of chairs fetched in
From nearby houses, and the undertaker,
In black Prince Albert and glum cleric air,
Whispers the proper order of their seating.

The sermon tells, in simple sentences
Touched with a note of rhetoric here and there,
The woman's sweet, maternal sacrifice
Throughout a rigorous, uncomplaining life,
And magnifies the melancholy hours
With deep emotion and huge thoughts of death;
And when he closes with a prayer for those,
The nearest and the dearest of the circle,
The helpless sobs of sorrowing hearts break out
In wails that drown the Bible words of hope.
The undertaker slowly waves his hand
And softly bids the neighbors pass around

To view their loving sister's last remains.
The carriages move off behind the hearse
In careful order of priority;
While in the rear the neighbors of the village
Trudge pensively and once again revisit
The plot where their own kin return to dust.

A few weeks later comes a courteous letter
With entries totaling four hundred dollars.
The bent old father whitens as he reads
This mortgage on his future life and home;
A heaviness draws down his face, the light
Departs, and silence weightier than speech
Enwraps him like a prison where one goes
To serve a lonely term of bitter years;
And in a scrawling hand he makes reply,
Signing the paper which he finds within—
Surrendering his last, lame, broken days
To ruthless perpetuity of debt.

The Sailboat

"I am a sailboat on life's racing waves
Beneath green headlands and a sapphire sky.
The motorboats rush by me with a roar
And kick up a commotion in the brine
Around me everywhere. I rear and toss
And lose all headway, fretted by the chop
These jiggling packets stir up on their rounds
From crowded island wharfs to fishing towns,
Shaking their sooty sterns at craft like me
Who want to keep the lanes of ocean white
With never-ending stretch of blooming canvas.

"When storms arise and turn the ocean's blue
To copper tints that strike the heart with fear,
And dark green squalls come hurtling from the west,
My pilot lets the anchor go, and furls
With care my flapping, rattling, bellying sails

And arm in arm we ride the tempest out
In land-locked harbors walled with evergreen.

"And longer still I wait when out at sea
I find myself upon the silken swell
Becalmed—no cloud above, reticulate ocean
Far as eye can reach on every hand.
Sleek porpoises, as black as naval guns,
Disturb the stillness with their stifled wheeze;
A crying sea gull flaps serenely by,
And driftwood, floating with the eddying tide,
Looms up, entwined with seaweed parched and brown,
Stirring my wonder as it drops astern,
Till down the channel out of sight it glides,
Leaving me in a stilly, passive mood
Upon the calm sea-prairies of repose.

"But when the air springs up and tells the shrouds
In scarce-felt whispers from the purple tide
The coming of a spanking southwest breeze,
My master spreads completely every stitch
Of canvas, takes the helm, away I spin
Along the slapping waves, my sails bulged out
In rounded fullness gloriously white;
The foam crest, boiling, bubbling at my bow,
Sings sailor chanteys to my pilot's ear,
And I am free and happy as the wind
That drives me as it drives the happy birds
Along the lime-green gullies of the sea.

"And now I reap reward for biding time
Through hurricane and blistering hours of calm;
The chugging motorboats with plunging strength
No longer do I envy; all good speed
I wish them as they sputter down the bay.
I heave to at my mooring and my sail
At sunset is a broad, white, flowing ribbon
Upon the pink neck of a gold-haired girl
Touched by soft breezes, as my pilot bends
The hawser on and leaves me for the night,

Clasped to the lips and bosom of my love,
The rhythmic, breathing lady of the tides."

Haunted

There are strange noises around an old house at
     midnight,
When our minds are most awake.
Are they the forgotten owners coming back to make
     themselves felt,
And throw off the oblivion to which we have so care-
     lessly consigned them?

The shutters make a breathing sound
As if some faithful hired man
Had come back, and were using them for lungs.

A faint tinkle, as of iron, floats up from the cellar:
Is it the stirring of a former tenant
Trying to shake off death's chains?

A rooster calls out loudly two hours before his time.
I imagine he is greeting his old master
Who is rustling the leaves
Walking among the hollyhocks by the garden wall.

A bubble of earth resounds far off,
Like the removal of a bung from a cask of old wine.
Is it the echo from one of earth's haunted places,
Opened to let ghosts wander free?

The floor intermittently creaks overhead.
Perhaps it is some spirit walking in the attic
To see if his childhood playthings are still there.

There is a wailing in the wind
Around the corner of the house—
A wailing as of the crying of gulls,

Or the sighing of children who have been whipped
    and sent to bed hungry.
Is this a sighing protest against being sent to the
    bed of death,
When earth itself is so lovely?

What are these strange noises that cluster around
    an old house at midnight?

The Denuded Island

"Why have you taken away
My children, and left me deserted,
With only the water beneath
Shuddering, bitterly chill?

"Alas! must I silently stand
Cold and gray and bare,
A rock in a bleak cold ocean
Awaiting the endless erosion
Of the myriad, long-lagging centuries?
I who was once as fresh
As the spruce trees growing in clumps
Down to the water's edge,
Spruces that kept the wind
From blowing the puffs off my back,
Luring the birds to my dwelling
In the first warm inkling of spring:
The glossy, blue-black crows
Cawing out of the branches;
The chickadees scattering music
As if the limbs of the trees
Were strings in a finely tuned orchestra,
And they the official musicians;
The fish hawks whom nobody ventured
To shoot at lest bad luck attend him,
Circling around at low tide,
Diving into the eelgrass,
Bringing out mussels and clams,
Dropping them down on the rocks

48

For their young ones hungrily crying
In branches of fir and dead spruces.

"Even the fish hawks are gone,
And I am left gray and alone,
Gray as the aged gulls
That cry as they circle around me,
Gray as the voice of the loon,
The saddest note of the shoreline.

"O choppers and builders of weirs,
Importunate seekers of pulpwood,
Why could you not have spared
My younger, willowy children
From whom I could have reared
A forest like that you have stolen,
A forest of evergreen spruces
And birches as crisply white
As a young girl's soft round shoulders;
Suddenly opening groves
Like naves of Gothic cathedrals,
For sailors to look at and brood on,
For fisher boys rowing their sweethearts
Toward Sunday embraces at twilight
In nooks of green trees and gray ledges?
O how could you strip me of tree-light,
And leave me a rock in the ocean
With never a spruce or an alder
To soften my rest through the ages?"

The Abbie S. *Loads Paving*

"The *Abbie S.* is heading toward the harbor
For one more load of paving." At this word
We joined the gang that sauntered toward the wharf,
Caught flounders, went in swimming, skipped flat stones,
Or listened to the golden cadences
Of old Tom Wiley's stories: how the boys
Of other days ran off and went to sea
At fourteen years, and how they made

The South Sea Islands in a raging storm,
Were blown away, and forced to spend a month
Among the palm trees in a blue lagoon
Where naked cannibals ran out and in.

Old men like Tom had always gone to sea
On huge square-riggers; they detested schooners
Far more than we abominated barges;
And one, who twitched a pirate's hardened mouth,
Whose eyes were bloody, and whose leathery fists
Were always clenched as if expecting trouble,
Who wore stout cowhide boots, the last red pair
To link our coast with days of Captain Kidd,
Growled out that morning in a frightening tone,
While this three-master glided up the cove:

"I hate these homely hookers scooting round,
Pretending they're as good as old-time ships,
When them as knows can see they don't come up
In any way: they just ain't ships at all!
I always did steer clear of barkentines,
And morphodite brigs, and hookers such as these.
Why, these fresh gaff-and-boom things rile me so
I don't know how to speak the way I feel:
I'd rather be hanged on board a square-rigger
Than die a natural death on board a fore-and-after!"
By this time *Abbie S.* had downed her jibs
And topsails; we could hear the captain shout
His orders, see the sailors run the deck—
Among them four resilient, shambling Negroes,
The first to fill our childish eyes with wonder;
They trimmed the sheets to rhythm, coiled up rope,
And stopped to see her luff into the wind.
She ranged too far ahead, till, at the wharf,
Big hawsers were flung out, made quickly fast,
And, like a wild horse at a snubbing post,
Shuddered in her tracks, and came to rest.

The old men looked her over, stem to stern,
And made no outward comment, but their eyes
Flared wistful, mellow gleams, betraying memories

Of balmy southern seas with full-rigged ships
Cleaving the blue, beneath the Southern Cross.

As these gray sea dogs scanned the far horizon,
Two noisy, high-wheeled dumpcarts rumbled and rattled
Hauling the paving to the dock for loading.
Four stout longshoremen, biceps strong as cables,
The color of the *Abbie S.*'s spars
Gray stone-dust sprinkled on their arms and eyebrows,
Kept tally, hurling blocks down iron chutes
While all around the rickety, clattering hubbub
Drove frightened sea gulls from the harbor bar.
The lanky teamsters on the dumpcarts yelled
Commands that carried echoes half a mile;
And when the pin was loosened from the dumpcart
The deafening crash of stone startled the horses
That pranced about switching their bushy tails.
The driver, yelling "Whoa!," put back the pin
And joggled off to haul another hundred.
The din of counting went on endlessly.
The grind of wheel rims on the narrow wharf
And frequent crash of dumping from the high carts
Mingled with granite-crunching thuds resounding
In hard metallic thumps along the stone chutes.

Five days the work went on; noon of the sixth,
A choppy high tide lapping over the gray rocks,
The deck was cleared for getting underway.
Clack-clack, the blocks replied, as the halyards tightened;
And, foot by foot, the sails arose to greet
The warm west wind, heavy with scent of orchards.
The sails bulged out; the captain grew self-conscious,
And left the wheel to inspect the water barrels;
The heavy hawsers, cast off, hit the water,
And bit by bit the hooker gathered headway.
We watched the foam lashed up amid the green
To darker, swirling green beneath her stern.
The wharf was jammed with chattering festive people
Who waved their hats and hands and handkerchiefs;
Dull men grew witty, and the eyes of all
Were burnished like worn linings in the stone chutes.

The crew doffed caps and swung a last good-by
As the *Abbie S.*, winged out, moved past the headland,
And boldly plunged to meet the Atlantic gales,
Blending one more stone carrier with the horizon.

Today these paving quarries all are stilled.
The blacksmith shops, where once the tinkle of iron
Resounded *clink-clank-clink* the seasons through,
Are drooping to a rusty, bronze decay.
The *Abbie S.*, dismantled and worn out,
Asleep upon the flats where all is silent,
Makes picturesque designs for city artists,
While vessels of her vintage now give way
To ugly barges bearing coastwise freight,
For fair white sails no longer dot the ocean.
And we, like Tom's gray crew a lap before us
(The last one now at rest upon the hillside
Beneath a granite anchor for his headstone),
Bewail the coming in of barges towed
By grimy tugs; we long to see white canvas
And rigging looking delicate at sunset,
When lacelike shadows flicker on the water,
And fifty vessels lying in the harbor
Transmute themselves at dusk into a fleet
Of fairy, phantom ships whose marvelous spell
Once more flings back an answer to man's craving
Confronted by the deep call of the sea.

Autumn's Country

I

New England is autumn's country:
Spring is there, to be sure,
With lady-slippers,
And trailing arbutus
As delicate as robins' twilight singing;
Winter, too, is there,
As hard and bleak as Stoic philosophy;
Gay summer, with its wonder world of daisies,
And fragrance rising warm from meadow haystacks.

But autumn is the land's true season:
In autumn the boys from a thousand coast towns
Stand on the creek banks fishing for smelts
Whose amber scales to them are fairer
Than the golden nuggets of Alaskan mines.
In autumn the young men along the coast
And the middle-aged men whom the season makes boys
Take from the racks above the kitchen doors
Their well-oiled guns and put out before dawn
To the brown shining rocks where the gray coots are feeding.
In autumn the big-game hunters
Hear the call of the deep Maine woods,
The call of the bull moose snorting,
The frightened sniff of the graceful deer,
And the evanescent but enduring call
Of dappled sunlight under nut-brown trees
Around a campfire at supper time,
With the curling smoke of the briar,
And the luxury of bodily weariness
Promising unbroken sleep.

The purple haze above her golden treetops
Is deep as the blue of her fringed gentians,
Her delicate hardwood leaves are red like wine,
Or bronze, like her burnt-orange sunrises,
Or brown like her newly made cider,
Or green-gold, like October sunsets.
The rustle of falling maple leaves
Strikes my ear like the rustle of silks
At the smiling approach of a woman
Whose comeliness silvers a household;
And the tapestries over the lawns,
With the pungent aroma that rises
From fires all over the village,
Lead my fancy away to the colors,
Burnt incense, and watch fires of Homer.

II

Deeper still, autumn is the spirit's true mood in
    New England.
It appears in the souls looking out from the eyes

Through lids piped about with brown pigment,
Of her most patrician women,
Smiling decorously
As they pass in their broughams and twin sixes
The brownstones of Commonwealth Avenue,
Or read the *Atlantic*'s prim pages
As devoutly as ever their fathers
Perused the great psalms of the Bible.
It appears in the crisp, shielded lives
Of her straightforward, neatly toned daughters
Whose manner has the charm of a squirrel
Gracefully sitting on a gray rail fence,
With brown paws uplifted together;
And whose apprehensive glances
Are as startled as partridges
Beating brown wings through a thicket
At the stealthy approach of a hunter.
It appears in the speech of her hardy young men
Whose voices visit my ear
Like the brooks of her mountain streams singing:
Harvesting crops of their fathers,
And reaching maturity late,
Like the flowers of northern New England.
Clearest of all it appears
In her old men lanky and brown,
Like her lawns keeping green through November,
When the year's twilight surrenders its leaves,
And the boughs on the sky-tinted water,
In an atmosphere blue as the ocean,
Have the crispness of delicate etchings.

III

Gray were the souls of the Mayflower Pilgrims
Who grimly set foot on the gray beach at Plymouth;
But the Promised-Land-light in their faces
Mingled the gray with mosaics of gold.
Their sortie on earth was a long, gray tunnel
With a gleam of light at the heavenly end.
An autumn-leaf dignity mellowed their language,
And mellowed the speech of their serious followers,

Scattered over a rocky soil,
Coloring a nation's heritage.

The towering soul of stout Jonathan Edwards,
Born to the stature of Dante or Milton,
Lapses from spring, the true season of poets,
And shrinks in the blight of autumnal New England:

> "I walked abroad alone
> In a solitary place in my father's pasture,
> And as I was walking there
> And looking upon the sky and clouds
> There came into my mind so sweet a sense
> Of the glorious majesty and grace of God
> That I know not how to express;
> A calm sweet abstraction of soul
> From all the concerns of the world;
> And sometimes a kind of vision
> Of being alone in the mountains,
> Or some solitary wilderness,
> Far from all mankind,
> Sweetly conversing with Christ,
> And wrapt and swallowed up in God."

IV

Or turn to the summer-ripe best of New England
And sniff even there the cool musk air of autumn
Like twilight-cool winds in the mid-heart of day.

Climb the fresh trails alluring to Emerson
As he bade good-by to the lowland and plain,
Leaving regretfully haunting cathedrals,
Gloomily aisled, dimly monastic;
At rest in the shade of a tree on Monadnock
Reading the mystical pages of Swedenborg,
Till darkness and evening star clustered around him;
Down from the mount with long paces through underbrush
He strode like an afterglow flame on red maples,
And standing in the torrent of Civil War rages
Uttered his lucid pronouncements to men.

Autumn severity creeps through the pages
Of Henry Thoreau, the exquisite doubter;
Barren of foliage his slim, graceful branches,
Nakedly brilliant their shadow-green bark
Against the frosty pink air of late autumn twilights.

V

The fall spirit over these coast towns,
As thick as the myriad leaves
At the foot of her oaks or red maples,
Stirs with a mood as much different from summer's
As the sigh of the wind in November branches
From the rippling of zephyrs through leaves of July.
Men return, catlike, again to these harbors
To be crooned to in age by the voice of the sea;
And the kelps and the rockweed, the old mother's jewels,
Though tinted four seasons an iodine brown,
Only reach to the height of their crystalline luster
When the October sun sluices off the gold nuggets
Of a thousand red cliffs in a clean-up of beauty.

VI

Land of waving goldenrod and lovely russet apples,
With little cedars on your slopes and driftwood on your shores;
Land of blue-fringed gentians and a million purple asters,
Land of bright red astrakhans and spice-brown groves of spruce,
Lovelier in age than in the vigor of your springtime—
Land of quiet tragedies and quiet brave repressions,
I know the light upon your face that only soul can bring;
And though you straggle far behind your zealous Western
    brothers,
Whose steps are firm, whose voices stout, whose plunging
    ventures carry
Success in every plunge and push a pathway to the stars—
For mine the fiber of your soul when facing life's illusions,
For mine the mood within your heart at noonday of Thanksgivings,
For mine your handsome, neat old age, the grandeur of your spirit,
That has matched your matchless autumn with an Indian Summer
    soul.

INNER HARBOR

Taking away the Banking

When March winds carried prophecies of June,
And gray days were no longer winter-killed,
We all went out and worked till afternoon
To take the spruce-limb banking off, and filled
The air with shouts, heaping what soon would be
A bonfire blazing by the willow tree.

We tugged at big ends of the bottom brush,
The small ends as reluctant to let go
As winter was himself, although the rush
Of warmth, once started, was an overflow
Of sunny days, bluebirds, and brooklets racing
Like children from worn mothers, tired of chasing.

We found that spring already underneath
Had started on his work; the light-brown grasses
Were flaunting spots of green, the little teeth
Of mice and snouts of worms had chiseled passes—
Worms we sent wiggling as a tempting cud
For hungry flounders coming out of mud.

O there were ugly days enough to come,
With rain and sleet and April flurries of snow,
Big winds that moaned and made the wires hum,
And neighbors calling out, "We told you so";
But looking on it now I think the days
We coaxed the spring along, and felt the rays

Of March intensify the balsam smell
In those green boughs, and saw the underpinning
Exposed once more, and children run pellmell
To hunt for crocuses, set fancies spinning
More rapidly than blooming hours of May
When all the hills of God kept holiday.

The Stallion

A chestnut stallion rising from the sea,
And clambering up a chestnut-colored ledge
On sinewy glossy legs that trembling slipped
Through rockweed in the crevices—his breast
Expanding and contracting like a wave,
His eyes forked lightning in a head of thunder—
Loomed high against the eastern rim of light
One August morning ninety years ago
When miles of water in Penobscot Bay
Lay tangled in the lazy summer sun.

The startled fishermen in yellow dories,
Feeling no mortal horse could tread that waste,
Gazed at each other while the color left
Their cheeks, the cod lines burned their hands;
Then peered across the dreaded spot once more,
Mouth open, till their wrinkled, red-rimmed eyes
Surrendered to the glimmer on the sea;
And stories they had heard old captains tell
Of weird sea serpents swimming round their hulls
As long as main booms and as brown as kelp,
At sunset when the ocean held its breath
And not a sound was stirring save the ripple
Of tiny waves flecking the copper plate
Beneath the figurehead—came crowding back
Into their credulous minds, . . .
But no one plucked up courage to speak out.

The white gulls, hollering, scattered from the ledge
As if they shared the terror of the men
Who, fearing earth might roll up like a scroll
Glanced north and south to find the rolling blue
Smoother than common and more streaked with foam;
A clamshell-colored stretch of morning sky,
With here and there a white patch leaning down
To see itself reflected in the water;

The only sound abroad an ocean bubble
Breaking far off with echo like swamp thunder—
And all the bay unchanged: the horse alone
Standing like some great statue wrought in bronze.

The Cove

When evening tide came rising with the moon
Out of the east and overflowed the cove,
Lifting the rockweed from a languid swoon,
And printing on its surface every grove

Of spruce and birch that stood along the shore
In shadows that transformed the leaves and boles
To antique etchings signifying more
Than blue Madonnas crowned with aureoles—

That was the cove's most captivating hour:
Pacing its banks we watched the Pleiades
Come up like meadow rue and palely flower—
My youthful passion flowering like the trees

That yearned above the cove, but never once
Stooped close enough to kiss the tide's smooth face;
So I with you—ah, did I seem a dunce?
The moonlight ate my passion every trace:

There was the subtle rent, the fissure fine:
The cove, the bond that welded us together;
Yours were the rocks and trees, the shadows mine;
Our harvest moon is white with winter weather.

And yet the cove allures when moonrise peeps
Over the tops of spruces—but a chill
Into the caves, and trees, and water creeps—
And my heart flares a little—then grows still.

Midsummer

Loafing on Maine's red rocks inside a harbor,
I hear the sea gulls like the sound of bagpipes
Across the blue-green stretches of cool water.
Then silence heaps itself as if some golden
Invisible moon far off beneath the ocean
Were hoarding up the flowing tides of quiet
That linger in these spruce-encircled inlets.

The lesser notes that ripple on the silence,
Intruding, yet not harsh nor melancholy,
Like wavelets shushing on white sandy beaches,
Or clink of bell buoys over sunken ledges,
Are gentle overtones to sea gull music
Echoing up the shore like haunting bagpipes
Across the sunlit slopes of dancing water.

Aged Ninety Years

The loneliness of her old age flashed clear
The day her body took its pilgrimage
Out of the little house where she had lived
Into the sunless house of brick-red dust.

The darkened room was empty, save for ghosts
Of those she loved who hovered near the place,
Unseen, but felt, trying familiar chairs.

Impassioned grief for those who die in youth—
The grief that holds the village in a mood
As spellbound as a frozen Arctic river—
Was absent here; and only vague relief,
Mingled with tenderness like that which flows
From soft wet mornings after autumn rains,
Relief of water lilies in a bowl,
Entered the quiet room where thin white hands
Were folded long and limp across her breast.
No throng of people followed to the grave,

62

A handful merely, these not friends of hers,
But of a daughter who watched over her
Throughout her failing years and closed her eyes,
Wishing perhaps a score of times the end
Might hasten on for respite to them both.

Within the half-forgotten ancient plot
The choking weeds and cemetery moss
Were blotting out the old New England names—
Seth, Adoniram, Hepzibah, Desire—
And curtaining the broken marble slabs.

Leaving the last grave in the double lot,
They turned their faces toward the flaming west
And felt the spirit of the autumn sunset
Put gently out its hand to push away
The specter of oblivion whose shade
Was stalking through these gray, neglected stones,
Foreshadowing like a winter night the hour
In which the proudest plinth the yard could boast
Would sink, like her, in chilly arms of earth.

Advice to a Clam-Digger
(An American Georgic)

Go when the friendly moon permits the tides
To drop far out at early morn or eve;
When eelgrass lies in windrows on the flats.
And rockweed lays its khaki counterpanes
On barnacles that cling to sunken ledges;
Seek out a place where mud-enameled sand
Looks like a colander whose holes emit
Little salt-water geysers when you step;
Then, facing shoreward, dig till you become
A lame and muddy partner of the cove.

Marvels undreamed of suddenly unfold
The secrets they have kept concealed so long;
The rancid mud clams whose white shells betray

A worthlessness within, like beggar's gold,
Or empty conch shells farther up the beach;
The iridescent clamworms blue and green
With escalading red and yellow fringes,
Like Chinese dragons whose soft tentacles
Expand, contract, and writhe in oozy slime;
Long-buried whores' eggs; razor fish with shells
Brown as old ivory and smooth as glass;
Or soggy timbers from a derelict
Who left her oaken bones upon a ledge
In some northeaster forty years ago.

You soon discover that the big returns
Lie nestled near the rocks that dot the cove;
Dig slowly there, lest you should break their shells,
For at a single forkful three or four
Will lay white buttocks bare before your eyes.
Protruding heads that keep a passage clear,
Aware of you, will scramble for their homes,
Spraying your eyes and face with stinging brine,
Engendering illusion that the shells
Are burrowing a fathom deep in mud.
Their flight is aided by the tousling in
Of saucy waters playing hide-and-seek
In every drain and crevice of the flats,
Laughing at your attempts to keep them out,
And salvaging dominion for the sea.

Your roller full, haul up your rubber boots
And wade into the green and golden cove
Where little flounders flit beneath your feet.
Pull bits of rockweed from vermilion cobbles
And wash the thick-accumulated mud
From off your hoe handle; then souse your hod
And watch the shades of blue intensify:
The sparkling freshness on the dripping shells
Which disappears as suddenly as dew
From violets or daisies in the sun,
Will teach you why the Indian long ago
Used these fair shells for ornaments and wampum,
And piled them in the self-same spot for years,

Until his heaped-up mounds were monuments
Where all spring wanderers might come and camp.

Fail not before you leave to glance around
And view the low-tide pageant of the shore:
The apprehensive manner of a gull
Who sits with white breast bulging to the breeze,
And flashes right and left his sulphur bill;
The slower movements of the pearl-gray crane
Who stands in eelgrass on a single leg,
Surveys the fishing prospects, then moves on,
To light again, survey, and move once more,
Till he has sounded out the channel's length;
The yellow bubbles on the flood tide making;
The dignity of rusty-iron rocks
Studded with bands of sharp white barnacles;
The breakers, if the wind blows hard off shore,
That chase each other on the sunken reefs,
And spout like white whales on an Arctic sea;
Or, if the earth be hushed to twilight calm,
The violet, dark wine, and purple tints
That crown the flowing surface of the tide.

New England

Inside, gray smoke curls up;
Outside, white flakes troll down
Against bare maple trees
In an old New England town.

Earth lags, securely sealed
To any tropic gust,
Like a plain New England heart
Indifferent to lust.

Nestled in little hills
A waning breed of men
Birth-date their headstones—
What is left then?

Vacation Morning

The voices of men talking on the water
Wake me at cinnamon dawn.
Out of the city last night,
Weary of grinding noises,
Longing for sleep and rest,
I came and threw myself down;
But the silence crowding round me
Here in this quiet room,
The honeysuckle climbing up the porch
Tossing fragrances in through the window,
The sea gulls haranguing the sunrise,
And, humming like bees near the casement,
The voices of men talking on the water,
Have showered me over and entered
Into my body and mind
Like the rippling drip from their oars
Returning in pearls to the cove.

In the cool of the early morning,
Watching the great sun turn,
Watching the flood tide move
And reach long finger tips
Into the cut-grass patch
Under my window sill,
I dreamily wonder why
Cities that nightmare the world
Must drown out these pastoral voices,
Voices blending with sunrise
Scattering peace on the waters.

Thanksgiving

I

Thanksgiving!
And I, far away
From the shores of Pilgrim New England,

66

In the sun-baked heights of the West,
Ponder the smoke from my pipe
Till into its rings of beech blue
Seacoast pictures are set,
Gilded like coves at dawn
On the kelp-fringed coast of Maine.

II

I stroll again along the shore
Kicking away the snow on the tawny marsh grass,
Listening to the voice of the sea.
The tide is ebb, and the khaki rocks
Come out like crack battalions
Ready for festive maneuvers
On the yellow-green field of the bay.
Round them animated breakers
Gayly toss their white-lace fringes;
And the sunlight sparkling on the rockweed
Close to the water's edge
Kindles the periwinkles into radiance,
Dazzling the foam where the headland
Plights troth with the changeable tide.

III

From the windy, wave-battered beach,
With its iodine odor of kelp
And its salty infiltrate of freshness,
I enter a little clump
Of birch trees and chocolate spruces,
Whose limbs droop over the path
With a whispering, calm
Benediction,
And whose roots stream away through brown turf
Knotting themselves in a cluster
Like myriad-branched candelabra
On moss-draped granite altars
Beneath the blue nave of the sky.
In the distance a church bell is calling;
But the chant of the wind through the thicket
And the incense from boughs bid me linger.

From her downstairs room grandmother hobbles
Mumbling half to herself
The comforting words of a psalm.
The mother glows to see the large brood
Gathered contentedly round her;
The father, his pride held in leash,
Warns the boys to remember their manners,
As he raps the board twice for a blessing;
Silence, and all through the circle
Runs a thought for their fathers' God
Whom they awkwardly feel they have slighted.

At the secular end of the table
Two sons on vacation from college,
Bantering, cry for the wishbone;
In their faces a voluble joy,
Only matched by a flush in the mother
They long to show love for—instead
They garnish with praises her turkey,
And Mary, the stay-at-home sister,
Seizing her one autumn chance
For a glimpse into less stony pastures,
Proposes, "Let's go on a sleighride
And dance in the New Harbor Grange Hall."
The curve of her neck as she turns
To hold back the protests of grandma
Flashes ruddy memories
Of a long-buried, favorite sister;
And smoldering glances reveal
Yearnings—infinite longings—
Flickers that die in the embers,
Choked by the slag of restraint.

V

Twilight thickens over the New England landscape;
Snow begins falling, adding a hush to the spirit
        of the late afternoon.
The gray and white shading sculptures a more
        intimate world;
Heaven is nearer earth than we had ever suspected:

The gradually falling snow seems to come from the
    weather-worn roofs of heaven
Whose eaves encircle the earth to shelter her
    fugitive children.
Through the gnarled limbs of an old apple tree
    I look again:
Big flakes are now falling, the earth is still,
And a warmth filters into the dusk enveloping
    stone walls and fences.

Harbor

Apart from pull and haul of modern aims,
Beyond all other spots on earth I know,
This harbor in the early morning glow
Of July sunlight presses me with claims
No city street can match: the boats that bask
At anchor in the bight, the lobster car
Bleached out upon the sand, the smell of tar
The sun tries out of herring nets, the flask
As toggle on a lobster pot not far
From ledges where the quiet wash of waves
Incessantly beats out its varying tone;
And out across the mussel-studded bar
The sound of sea gulls reaching umber caves
Mingles its music with the ocean's own.

Restoration
(To Margaret, aged five)

You ran up to the nursery of my heart,
Pulled click the iron latch and tumbled in;
Tore instantly three boxes wide apart,
That held a broken doll, a wreck of tin—
Once glittering train of cars—a twisted pup
With trembly tail that used to be the friend
I slept with every night; you stood these up
With magic hands, till I could see the end

Of all their imperfections in the spell
Your smile worked out before my wondering eyes;
The doll smiled, too; the cars went ding-dong-bell
And rushed off round the track; the big surprise,
However, came when that long-lost white Fido
Barked in his dear old way and cut a dido.

Impressions

These entered into me and shaped my dreams:
The full triumphant buoyance of flood tide;
A wooded cove streaked with the low moon's beams;
A little island where white sea gulls cried
My drowsiness astir, and perched to ride
With schooners that indulged the wind's desire:
Calm spots on choppy seas; a terrified
Northeaster rousing moods that lifted higher
Than pushing waves; the reminiscent fire
In eyes of sailors who had plowed the main
On full-rigged ships where mutinies and dire
Atlantic gales from Montreal to Spain
Had filled them with adventure glowing bright
As brass rings in their ears by candlelight.

Margins

The birds frequent the entrance to the wood,
And fish patrol the edges of the shore;
March breezes that anticipate May's mood
And nuzzle round torn fences token more
To me than mid-May's lilac-scented noons;
A friend who leaves me at my inmost shrine
Is dearer far than one who importunes
From me the secrets I would still keep mine;
And even lovers stale not who retreat
From chambers in love's mansion where alone

Their loved ones sit determined to defeat
Gregarious hours challenging their own—
Aware that half the secret of a star
Is grace to know the sun's heat from afar.

Manse

Post office, general store, and barber shop
Were not enough to keep Manse quite contented,
So long had he been used to mackerel seines.
The rippling ruffle of a school at play
Toward evening set his pulses pounding harder
Than anything on earth or on the sea;
And hence one could not call it wholly strange
One afternoon when fish were furrowing
The lilac harbor just beneath his window
While he was shaving Lawrence Tarreton,
The Middle Western novelist who came
Each summer to depict New England life
In its decline, for Middle Western readers—
One could not call it wholly strange that Manse
Without a word of warning left his charge,
With one cheek shaved, the other fully lathered
And made a beeline for his seine and dory.

He found the pod still playing near the surface,
Nor was his guess amiss about its size;
And when he drew the lead line taut, the fish,
Darting a silver-green from rim to rim,
Submerged the cork line till a grist got free.

Meanwhile our scribe, still in the barber chair,
Was sputtering to himself a choice array
Of epithets about the Maine coast natives
He used for character analyses
To round off corners in his clever stories:
Their charming inefficiency, their droll
And dilatory ways—this time, however,
The extenuating adjectives were dropped.

A neighbor seeing Manse knee-deep in fish,
His cheeks lit up with smiles and mackerel scales,
And in no hurry to bail out his catch,
Stooped down and whispered in his good ear, "Manse,
Did you by any chance forget a man
You left half-lathered in the barber chair?"
"My God, is he there yet? The pesky fool,
I thought he'd finish up the job himself."
And feeling like a husband who recalls,
Turning in home, an errand he forgot,
He pulled out one big boot and then another,
And took the short cut to the barber shop.

"What, you here yet? I didn't think you'd stay;
But you just wait till I wash off these scales
And change my rubber boots and I'll be with you."

Lawrence was too cut up to be amused;
The lather on his face was baked so hard
His cheek was wrinkled like an old dry fish skin;
He used a lower tone than ordinary
And put on all the dignity one could
In his predicament.
                                "What do you mean
By leaving me an hour in this chair?
I've always tried to treat you decently
And given you my custom; now you go
Without as much as saying *boo* and leave
Me waiting here an hour partly shaved.
No wonder you poor natives drag along
Year in, year out, and never get ahead,
You don't know what it is to tend to business;
Without the summer folks you'd almost starve."
Manse stopped his stirring with the shaving brush
As soon as the rebuke grew general;
He straightened up his six feet one of brawn
And looked straight in the eyes of Tarreton:
"You've gone 'bout far enough—I know I left
Without much ceremony—but if you think
I'd let a chance to get a school of mackerel
Slip through my fingers for a ten-cent shave

72

You're mightily mistaken—I'd 'a' thought
You'd have the sense to scrape the rest yourself.
And as for summer folks, just listen here,
They're spoiling half the people of this island;
Now all the girls must dress like rich men's girls;
The men turn into beggars figurin' out
An easy way to live off summer people;
Our women ain't content to stay at home,
But must take trips to Boston or New York:
I wish to God you'd never set your foot
Among us—and furthermore, for you,
I guess I won't shave off the other side,
It wouldn't be quite safe the way I'm feelin'."

Cordwood and Driftwood

The cordwood is a toiler
Coated with miry clay
Round whom the clematis of age
Has twined a robe of gray:
The driftwood is a poet
With a home in the western skies,
And over his beach-lit fire at night
Dreams sputter within his eyes.

The cordwood, somber-colored—
Gray-green, blue-black, and brown—
Has limbs chopped clean by the woodman's ax,
For the journey into town;
The driftwood is silvered as white as a bone,
And hard as a walrus' tusk,
There are knots untrimmed on each eelgrassed limb,
And phosphorus there at dusk.

The cordwood loves the haunts of men
In the gray North Temperate zone,
Curls up and warms the shoulder blades
Of folk whose dreams are flown;
The driftwood steers for the Behring floes,

And the Indian Ocean's breast—
A tramp of the tides, untamed he rides
On a more than earthly quest.

Thelma Maloney

She closed the tale of *Dora Thorne* to dream
Of balls where counts and dukes in velvet capes
And glittering swords swept broad-brimmed hats across
Their breasts for tribute to her comeliness,
Fencing with one another to secure
Her smile in one brief waltz across a hall
Made beautiful by ladies long since dead.
With *Ishmael* she rode to hounds and viewed
The charm of English country lanes; her own
Peculiar charm impelling men to stay
Behind and flatter her in courtly speech
Till envious dames acknowledged her as queen.

The rubber boots of Edgar clomping in
Made thunder for these lightning words, "My God,
Ain't you begun to get my dinner yet?"

She saw white yachts go up the bay in June
With brassworks luminous as minted gold,
Beneath whose awnings stylish ladies sat,
And on whose deck a pilot stood alert
In navy blue and white, binoculars
Each moment at his eyes—the bay as calm
As any mill pond resting in the hills,
With fragrance far more pungent, and a light
More dazzling than the glow of inland waters,
Both light and fragrance tempting one to dream
As she dreamed every sunny morning through,
Till ragged unwiped Johnny tugged her skirt
Whining, "I want a piece of b'e'd and butta."

When forty winters had depressed her lips,
Turning their blood-red warmth to parching white,

74

She built her dreams around the man who wore
The seamless robe and dared to speak of lilies.
The robe, clean teeth, and tones of him who came
To be their minister had set her mind
On loftier things; she loved to feel him near,
Drink from his youth the waters of a stream
That welled within herself and overflowed
Into a bank-erasing summer flood.
She told him all the troubles of her soul,
And strove to make his village church a place
Of warmth and cleanliness, acquiring zeal
To press religious duties on her mate,
At which he badgered her, swearing, "I'll see
Myself in hell before I humor you,
Or go to hear that pindlin' Christer preach."

Her last long illness came on suddenly,
And in its train delirium seized her mind
And held it to the end; she lived again
Her girlhood dreams, with music, castle walls,
White pleasure yachts against the forenoon's blue,
And glad church bells on Easter Sunday morning;
She felt the patient soul of Nazareth
Come close beside her bed and hold her hand,
With pressure like the preacher's soft white palm,
Guiding her through the low-tide caves of death;
And at the last she rallied for an hour
And heard two daughters snarling on the stairs,
Like midnight cats, disputing which should wear
The gown put by to serve her in the grave.

Fireplace

The roarings of the fireplace
Are the two and thirty breezes
That blew upon these oaks
When they marched up the hillside
Into the open sky.
        (Listen intently,

And you can distinguish
The gentle undulant airs
Out of the west and south
From the cavernous boreal blasts
Midwinter let loose from the north.)

The currents of sound beneath
This hurrying gusty roar,
Like cascades whispering through slender birches,
Are intercessions of the rain that fell
To slake the thirst of writhing roots and branches
After long days of drouth.
    (Hearken quietly,
    And the little falls
    You heard while walking in deep winter woods—
    A trickling procession of ripples—
    Will whisper to your eager ears again.)

The fragrances scenting the room
Are gathered-up tinctures of earth
That ran through the sap till they touched
The savory tips of long boughs—
Sprinkling leaves of October
With myriad nosegays of musk.
    (Inhale deeply
    These blossoming petals of smoke,
    And you can detect
    Incense the old brown mother
    Bottled within this rough bark
    To medicine winter with spring.)

The flames shooting out of these logs
Are skysails flapping at twilight,
Their backstays reaching earthward
Into each fiber and knot.
They reflect once again the bronze flare
From the waters tinting the west,
And lavish it over the hearthstone
To animate cold winter nights.
    (Look sharply
    And you can see squadrons

Skirting the coast of the sunset,
Where oaken spars lift topmasts
Into a topaz sky—
Squadrons laden with cargoes
For the warehouse of your dreams.)

Extenuating Circumstances

"Stand up and hearken unto an indictment
Returned against you by Knox County jurors;
Fred Gray with force and arms did break and enter,
Maliciously and with intent to injure,
Did injure and destroy the property
In Ezra Staples' pasture of great value,
To wit: one certain billboard or one hoarding
Which then and there belonged to Isaac Bloom:
Did feloniously steal and carry away
Against the peace and honor of the state
And statutes in such cases made and provided."

"What say you now, Fred Gray, to this indictment?"

"Yes, Judge, I'm under oath and have to plead
Guilty of tearin' down that big board sign;
But grant me leave to tell the Court just why—
There were extenuatin' circumstances.
The first fall days had just come on; the wind
Out of the north had made the bay deep blue,
And whitecaps on the cove grew prettier
Tryin' to match the edges of the clouds.
The beaten paths were growin' sunburnt brown
Like a youngster's hair when he is two or three
And goes bareheaded in the sun all day;
The first red leaves were dottin' roadside maples,
And I was goin' home one afternoon
Thinkin', as one is bound to in the fall,
How much the air smelled like red astrakhans,
When I looked up and spied that pesky sign
Defacin' thirty feet of pasture slope.

"I don't suppose a prettier stretch of land
Exists outside a storybook: beneath
A swamp of juniper and hackmatack,
Blue flag and yellow touch-me-not in bloom;
And little clumps of alder deep-sea green,
With cowpaths windin' in and out among them;
And up the slope gray birches ten feet tall,
With open places scattered here and there,
Where grass grows belly-high takin' the wind
And bendin' to it like a pleasure yacht
Before a spankin' breeze out in the bay;
And further back forests of pointed spruce
All jungle-thick and dark as ebony,
But gay enough when sunset marches through.

"That sign did not belong in such a place,
So I went home and muckled ax and saw
And made hawk's meat of it before the spell
Wore off. A neighbor saw me workin' hard,
And noticin' my steam up more than usual,
Stepped in and asked me what I was about.
I told him I had need of firewood
To check the fall chill creepin' round the house.
These were the circumstances in the case
They make no mention of in the indictment."

A Maiden Lady

"My heart is a dandelion blossom
Ripened to a soft, white, downy fuzz;
The wind from a man-cloud blows over me:
Every tendril of my being is as delicate as twilight;
And just as I am fluttering
To the ecstatic hope of a great consummation,
I am blown away."

The Ballad of the Sandpeep Ghost

The quest for gold was a passion old
When Jason sought the Fleece,
From the rank and file to the top of the pile
It has robbed mankind of peace.

Witness the tale of Polly Dan
Who lived on Bowers' Hill
With an indolent shirk who fled from work
But hunted and fished with a will.

On a lone shore road they met a Swede
With rods for finding treasure
Who told where Captain Kidd had sunk
Gold bullion out of measure.

Next morning Polly said to Dan
"Tonight us two will go
And dig beneath that pasture rock
Before the moon is low."

"But Polly, don't you know they killed
A man each time they hid
Them Spanish bars? A spirit guards
That gold for Captain Kidd."

"Well, we've been poor now long enough,
Half-frightened of your shadow,
You'll come with me tonight and dig
That gold there in the meadow."

At nine they took a spade and pick,
A lantern not yet lighted,
And crept so cautiously along
That both of them were frighted.

They lit the lantern, started in;
Dan picked and Polly spaded,
When suddenly a piteous cry
The pitch-black night invaded.

"The ghost is here! I'll dig no more,"
Cried Dan to ghost and spouse,
And shouldering the fatal pick
Leg-bailed it for the house.

A thousand yards, he stopped for breath,
The heart in his throat was stuck,
Making a noise like dump-cart wheels
Knee-deep in gravelly muck.

The stop was brief, for soon he heard
A wail behind his lug,
Some fiend of hell had broken through
That foot of earth he dug.

Again he ran, and running heard
The dead man's wail of wrath;
It drove his untrained, flabby legs
Like pistons on the path.

He staggered home, threw down the pick,
And shoved the small door in
Where shadows mingling with the cry
Made all his blood run thin.

Ten minutes more, old Polly came,
Turned up the lamp and heard
That ghost outside the window sill
Still wailing like a bird.

It was a bird; when morning cleared
The dark off everything
They saw the sharp end of the pick
Had pierced a sandpeep's wing.

Zeb Kinney on College Professors

I don't know why I asked him what he thought
Of that peculiar brand of summer folk

Who rusticate among us three full months
Of every year. Perhaps it was that all
The other topics had been grappled with,
Or, better, paddled with, for that was no
Fit morning to be grappling anything.
The northern sun lay lovingly along
The sloping ledges on the western bank
Of that still cove where most of us had loafed
The finest mornings of our lives away,
Discussing, smoking, whittling in the sun—
Brown ledges whose soft shade reflected warmth,
And held our bodies anchored to the field,
Our legs extending downward to the shore,
A sort of no-man's-land for loafing in.
The grass around these ledges, beaten down,
Had turned from green to tawny and lay flat,
Echoing that appeal one gets from paths
Leading from kitchen doors to pasture wells.
We sat and dozed together, rousing only
When little pollock flipped above the cove,
Or some bright burst of sunlight hit beneath
A sea gull's wing directly overhead,
When Zeb, whose ruminations held him still
For nearly twenty minutes, straightened up
Above his favorite forty-five-degree
Extent of relaxation on the ledge,
Jabbed for a broken lath to whittle on,
Cleared out his throat, and rid himself of this:

"Well, these professors that you ask about
Who come here every year are curious.
I s'pose it takes all kinds to make a world,
And none of us should be too heavy on
A neighbor, even if he don't belong.
Of course they don't belong, that's sure enough:
The smell of herrin' bait in George's skiff
Would knock the stoutest of them galley west;
And none of them appears to be real rugged.
When they go out to hand-line cod with me
They keep a-lookin' round at birds and boats
And colors on the channel—scursely one

Can ketch his share of cod—and never once
Has ary one of them hauled up his sleeves
And helped me gut a fish when we rowed in.
They read the books that other people don't,
And never talk about the books they read,
Leastwise to us; and some of them go in
And pound the typewriter three times a day,
Like I would go to meals; but what they write
Not one of us hears ary word about.
I figger out they write their heavy books
For one another, not for common duffers.
They play book-lairnin' games of hide-and-seek
As we play racin' with our motorboats
On August mornin's when the shedderin'
And weather has us all a-feelin' good.

"I peeked jest out o' curiosity
At some typewritten papers once upstairs,
And found it all about the big mistake
Professor Somebody in Germany
Had made in chapter four of his big book
On quails. I don't suppose that chap could tell
An early old-squaw from a patchhead coot.
Next thing somebody else will write a book
In which this squid will have *his* gills hauled out
For some mistake *he's* made; it's all jest like
A batch of kittens playin' with their tails.
They don't go out enough and let the sun
Beat down and make them look like other folks;
They shrink before us lobster-ketchers do,
And hate to have their children roll around
In dirt and mud, like every youngster should.
Of course they wouldn't take advice from me,
But I can see them gather barnacles
Like my old sloop out there in Lobster Cove;
When barnacles and eelgrass slow her down,
I haul her up and take the scraper to her;
That's what professors need—a good sharp scraper
To clean the rubbish off their garboards, clean
The gubber from their engine valves and pipes
To perk them up so they'll get back their sprawl.

"Here comes one now through Amariah's field
To see how we behave when we set here
And talk all mornin' long; he'll listen to us,
And then go back and tell how quaint we be.
It takes all kinds of folks to make a world."

Youth

The old men talked of Barney's place
Two miles or so away,
Near a gray, half-tumbled wharf whose face
Abutted on the bay;
There Barney sold big jugs of rum
Before my dad was born,
And there gay sailors used to come
And dance and drink till morn.

They talked of Shepherd's Island four
Or five miles up the reach,
Where the squire left each spring a score
Of lambs along the beach:
The older boys hauled up the sail
On a pinky painted blue,
And left me standing sadly pale,
Too young to join the crew.

And since that dawn taverns of ease,
With dancing, wit, and wine,
And voyages from Arctic seas
To Egypt have been mine;
But never found I sumptuous fare
To equal Barney's style
Nor famous landscapes anywhere
That shone like Shepherd's Isle.

Midwinter Calm

On a soft open day in midwinter
When elm trees in fawn-colored jackets
Etch delicate outlines and clear
On the whetstone blue of the air;
When limbs from young maples droop down
And dapple with shadowy tracery
The fronts of colonial houses,
Like shadow bands during the hour
The moon steals the gold from the sun—
The trees in this Puritan village
From the rough-shapen roots of wild oaks
Turning black as the snow melts about them
To the tips of tall birches that stretch
For a glimpse of their brother, the sky,
Breathe a tranquillity deeper
Than the leaf-blowsy quiet of June.

Think with what stillness and patience
Northern trees wait for the spring!
The brooks are so mute that the snap
Of a clean block of ice in the stream
(Clean but for grasses stuck through it)
Disturbs like the voice of a child
Crying out in the hush of church service;
And the neighborly town-meeting fathers
Spread out in the shoemaker's doorway
Reminisce and smoke together,
As if hibernation were useful
For men as for trees in midwinter.

In the Gulf Stream

At the horizon's four portals no land
Or sea gull to dim the blue air,
Crafty hammerhead sharks lying still
As gargoyles along our black beam,
A rose window lighting the west,

84

And a ceiling of Tyrian blue
Overhanging dark flagstones of blue.

Where the waves from the ship meet the waves
Of the bulky indifferent sea,
A green hill heaves up bursting forth
Into groves of luxuriant trees
Branching with silvery limbs
That dance in the beams of the sun,
And scatter each moment white leaves—
A glinting profusion of leaves.

Farther out heap the slow-rolling waves
With shadowy spots on each crest,
Caravans moving along
The ridge of a wide desert waste—
Caravans destined to bring
To island and continent shores
The full-flavored spice of the sea,
The slow-yielding pearls of the sea,
The Behemoth lift of the sea.

Like a giant grown sick of the globe
And pining for wings to escape,
The sea, as the sun wallows down
To his mandate beyond the red verge,
Combs the phosphorus waves of his hair,
Adorns in deep purple and pearl
His silken and flexible limbs,
As if he were saying, "O sun,
Take me out of this world as you sink
Into lilac-strewn regions beyond,
For the root of an herb growing there,
Can heal this great longing in me,
This vagabond longing in me."

Country Dance

A tone of expectation filled the store
Below the hall the evening of the dance;
The old men occupying broken chairs
And nail kegs they had grown accustomed to
Indulging in their after-supper smoke;
Aunt Fronie, sole proprietor and clerk,
Dodging as usual in a dark side room
Soon as the smoke screen of the men was laid
To join them in an unseen partnership:—
A ritual unchanged; but in the eyes
And voices of the men a something lurked
That made one think this special evening burned
To memories a half a century bright.
The young folks waiting for the dance to start
Impatiently trooped in and out and in,
And bashful boys from unfrequented wood roads
Who never ventured on the shiny floor
Laid in a grist of peanuts that would last
Throughout the festive evening. Presently
The tuning of a fiddle caught our ears
And up we went to join the "march and circle."
The fiddler in a greenish glazed frock coat,
Discarded doubtless by some minister,
Stood on the stage adjusting spectacles
To eyes of larkspur blue and full of luster
That shone beneath thick overhanging eyebrows
Like pools of water under beetling cliffs.
His hair, once brown as spills of Norway pine,
Was now three-quarters gray, faint-streaked with brown,
And shaggy as a ripe chrysanthemum.
His high cheekbones that tokened passion once
Disclosed a mellowness to match his smile—
And he was blest if gaiety of spirit
Deserves a place among the beatitudes.
His gayest manner bloomed when he called off
The movements of a popular quadrille:

> "Right hand to your partner, grand right and left;
> Sashay out and form a line;
> Turn your corners; . . . Forward and back;

86

Promenade; . . . You're doin' fine.
Ready once more, now, eight hands round;
Lead to the right, and do-si-do;
Swing in the center; . . . Ladies' chain;
Balance all; . . . That set's too slow!"

The village periscopes about the hall
Would keep sharp watch for any change of convoy
The girls had made since last week's "march and circle."
More carefully they scrutinized the walk
And manner of some middle-aged dame
Whose second blooming stirred her to improve
Her dress and toilet and relive once more
Impassioned hours of tempestuous youth.
A few had sought release without the blooming;
Despairing souls who heard the gnawing rats
Of misery invade their homes at night.
Determined to invoke forgetfulness
They thrust their chins out willfully and stormed
Their way through measures in a mood that told
Theirs was a losing fight, for happiness,
Like heaven, cometh not by violence.

Their fog of desperation scaled somewhat
Whenever the fiddler cleared his throat and sang:

"Oh, there was an old man and he had a wooden leg,
He had no tobacco; no tobacco could he beg;
And another old man as clever as a fox;
Always had tobacco in his old tobacco box.

"Said the man with the wooden leg, 'Give me a chew';
Said the man with the other leg, 'Darned if I do;
Save up your money and salt down your rocks
And you'll always have tobacco in your old tobacco box.'"

The peanut chewers, not unlike the gossips,
Sat slumped throughout the evening in a corner—
White pimples showing through the fuzzy down
Of sallow cheeks, and furtive eyes betraying
The badge of Onan: long they watched to see
Some gay girl's petticoat swing out too high,
A signal for a joke or vulgar story.
These were the gargoyles on the structure built

To yield the village gay and happy hours—
Far different from the striplings on the floor
Clapping their hands and beating out the tune,
Balancing a folk song back and forth
Till creaking could be heard among the rafters.
And some were there whose heads were barren hills
After a fall of January snow;
Others with infants stretched in smiling sleep
On brown settees that trailed around the room.
To all except the jealous and the old
The hours went zooming by on airy wings
That failed to open through the drudgery
Of six days at the sink or in the wherry.
And all too soon the strains of "Home, Sweet Home"
Set up a brief stampede among the couples
Till each lad found his lass, when all would go
Back to the store beneath where empty chairs
Now took the place of reminiscent men.

Outside the grinding of an iron tire
Against a wagon body backing round;
The village drunkard hooting at the moon
Mingled with "Good night, Joe," and "So long, girls";
Repeated click of Aunt Sophronia's latch;
Her last lamp hesitates—then flickers out;
And nothing more all night but moonbeams beating
On cold uncurtained windows of the hall.

Prayer Meeting

A little after seven Thursday evening
The remnant gathered in the meeting house
To pray once more the never-changing prayers,
And underrun once more the testimonies
The people of the village knew by heart.

The janitor, devoutly Christian Tom,
With sawed-off beard of bristles, always came
An hour before the time: for prayer, thought some;

For close communion with the weed denied
To those who publicly professed, thought more:
(The phrase the village used would never say
Quite what it was the remnant all professed:
A shibboleth, it served for those outside
To cover up their sins: "I know I'm far
From perfect, but then, I make no profession.")
Old Tom's profession on his bended knees:
"We now will have a comfortable waiting
With Thee, O Saviour, in Thy house today,
And pick ambrosial fruit from life's fair tree
Within the Paradise of God"—was known
To every schoolboy in the neighborhood.

Whatever Tom's design, Aunt Cal, who sat
As number two in that elect assembly,
Would always cap her clearing of the decks
By scrutinizing Tom's red stubbly beard.
"Cleanse Thou him" was often on her lips
At these preliminary skirmishes:
But truth compels one to declare that "cleanse"
Loomed higher in her mind than "secret faults,"
For she was neat past all tales of ablution:
The flowers on her bonnet trim as wax,
The black strings underneath in order tied,
The linen handkerchief in folds that lay
Exactly so; the tightness of her waist,
And even the gingham cover of her hymnbook,
Bespoke the immaculate altars of her spirit.

Another regular whose "doubts and fears"
Were never absent from her testimony
Lived on a wood road two miles out of town.
Her English peasant husband, finding rocks,
Too plentiful in Maine's reluctant soil,
Had clasped the fingers of John Barleycorn
To help him over these impeding bowlders—
And soon he found himself on slipperier ledges;
Came home one rainy night and drove his wife
Out of the house. There on the lonely road,
Depressed, she knelt in prayer like Saul of old,

Until she, too, beheld a heavenly light:
This was the burden of her testimony;
And in my mind I never see her now
Save as she looked on rainy Thursday evenings,
Her shawl about her head, with drops of water
Over her coal-black locks that shone like beads
Of pearl when rays of the swinging lamp
Lit up the gipsy shadows of her face.

The pride of all the group, though most of them
Held this like other prides should be suppressed—
A high-school girl walked down the middle aisle
Giving that aisle a moment's animation.
Her youth seemed an anomaly blooming here
In this antique collection of pressed flowers;
And her unfolding beauty white and gold
A more unique anomaly: her eyes
Were like the blue tints of Penobscot Bay
On sunny August afternoons; her hair
In two large golden braids adorned a back
Fit for the daughter of a Niobe;
And in her heart unformulated dreams
Gathered momentum struggling for expression
When she sang earnestly her favorite hymn:
>   *"I look away across the sea*
>   *Where mansions are prepared for me,*
>   *And view the shining glory shore,*
>   *My heaven, my home forevermore—"*
A hymn which showed she heard the rattling chains
About her in this dungeon of dry bones.
But half-and-half beliefs that sat so well
On more accommodating minds were not
For her; and while she covenanted with them
She kept a burnish on each heavy link
In this depressing chain of blank negation.
For her no playing cards or dances warmed
The heavy-hanging chill of winter hours;
The others frolicked while she sat apart,
Wistful, but never yielding lest she be
A stumbling block to those of frailer stuff;
And in her senior year when she was chosen

90

"Queen of the May" because her spirit shone
Fairer than other maidens of the county,
She wrestled long in prayer and then refused,
Because the May fete ended with a dance.

Old Deacon Work, wearing a stand-up collar
Whose corners never ceased to prod the folds
In his much-folded neck, leaned heavily
On a loud-thumping cane till he had reached
The front pew on the right aisle of the room,
In which he sank himself with blowing sounds,
Not unlike porpoises come up for air—
The neighbor dubbed it "blowing off his steam."
He rose to speak, or rather rose to mumble
And might be muttering darkest heresy
For all his hearers knew; then like a squall
He poured forth three or four explosive words
With vehemence and passion so intense
It still was hard to tell what he was saying:
"LORD JESUS CHRIST" was one he always boomed,
"ATONING BLOOD" another; after these
His shallop righted to an even keel
And glided on Gennesarets of calm.

A self-effacing seeker glanced around
Before he rose, to make sure no one else
Was pressing prior claims—though his intent
Bulked far more definite than promises
Of blessings on a gathered two or three.
The larger number there would never know
He used these meetings for an end that roused
Their Saviour to unmitigated rage
One morning as He wandered through the Temple.
He wisely knew a few were not convinced,
And always sought to soothe them with the text
Which told men to forget the things behind
And reach out hands for things that are before.
Evasively he tiptoed from the room,
Avoiding contacts with the few blunt souls
Who might have blurted out their inmost thoughts—
Went home to reckon column after column

Of interest on the mortgages he cherished,
Dipping his bony fingers late at night
Into a brown cigar box full of silver.

Two sisters whom the pastor always called
His "autumn leaves" could never quite make sure
What time sufficient grace would be vouchsafed
For them to testify; though one whose years
Were closer to the Psalmist's threescore ten,
More timid, had the stronger sense of duty;
And rubbing palm on palm half stooped, half stood,
And in words quavering up and down the scale
With coaxing intimacy said: "I feel
My Saviour has been with me through the week,
And I—I have a feeling He will be
With me and keep me faithful to the end.
I feel I need an int'rest in your prayers
That what I feel may grow in me and give
Me strength to stand and speak the faith I feel."
And though both sinners and believers smiled
They always ended on a note of praise,
Knowing the tender impulses that led
Her fragile steps from home to needy home.

Three-quarters through the hour pauses fell
That no amount of ingenuity
The pastor summoned could alleviate;
Though his resources were so heralded
With overtures of kindliness no man
Or woman there felt cymbals crashing loud
In orchestras of everlasting doom.
He took his silver watch out and began
To rub the crystal with his long right thumb
Until we used to fear the glass would break
Before our very eyes, leaving him rubbing
The minute hand toward longed-for half-past eight.
"There still is time," he always told his flock—
He might have said eternity for all
The help he gave the clock that ticked away
So slowly and so faintly on the wall
We often fancied it was running down.

92

"There still is time for you who have not spoken
To tell the old, old story of the Cross";
And one who felt he should declare his faith
Was in such torment he struck up the hymn:

> "I love to tell the story
> Of unseen things above;
> Of Jesus and His glory,
> Of Jesus and His love;
> I love to tell the story
> Because I know 't is true,—
> It satisfies my longing
> As nothing else can do.
>
> "I love to tell the story,
> 'Twill be my theme in glory,
> To tell the old, old story
> Of Jesus and His love."

More silences; more timid ones responding;
And in the wake of each, encouragement
Benign, expository cheer, and smiles
Of radiant approval that pronounced
"Well done" till those glued down past ever rising
Felt envy tinged with guilt toward those who spoke;
Nor could they shake the guilty feeling off
That they had jarred once more the crown of thorns
By keeping silence while the others told
Uncomfortably the comfort they had found
In wandering the pastures green where flow
The crystal waters of eternal life.

The welcome benediction. People stirred
And greeted one another cordially
But not effusively, though some who had
Ripe morsels to communicate could not
Hold back the eager glitter in their eyes.
A few young blades who lingered near the door
To see their sweethearts home were noisier
Than many thought quite proper in God's house;
And Tom the janitor was shooing people out
Like some old woman shooing hens she loved.

The farther off they went the louder rose
Their conversation; smiles broke into laughter,
And natural behavior once again
Resumed its normal course, as far indeed
As people lost in fogs of "Thou shalt not"
Could find a normal passage through the dark
Uncharted thoroughfares of human life.

Veterans

The square New England house
Blinks in the winter sunshine,
Like its outward-gazing companion
At rest on the spruce limb banking
When a tall white morning lays over
The world a garland of light.
Curling smoke from the chimney,
Like smoke from the graybeard's pipe,
Saunters lazily upward
And scatters in cobalt air.

Eighty New England winters
Have mortised the house to the landscape,
And buttressed the old man's spirit
To share its fate with the shadows—
His spirit grown familiar
With the breathing of these hills;
The hills for years expecting
The echo of his voice.
He will be waiting at ease
When the dark eclipse comes total,
On the interwoven green spruces
At the sunny side of the house—
His body leaning forward,
Hands clasped on the head of his cane,
Waiting at ease the call,
Though never quite ready to meet it,
For house and man to settle
Deeper still in the dust.

94

A Northeaster

For two bleak days the warning pennant red
Above a red square flag foretold the gale;
The louring storm clouds, torn to many a shred,
Patrolled the sky till the threatened sun grew pale;
Southwestern flurries shook the weathervane's tail
Before the churning sea went foamy white;
Then from the feared northeast arose a wail
Which whined its way to every bay and bight,
And darkness hung like smoke on the blue-black shore that night.

With clocks to punch the surfmen dragged their feet
To cliffs where keys were chained, embrowned with rust;
Their swinging lanterns, beaded thick with sleet,
Lit up black rubber boots against white crust;
Toward daybreak, in the calm that trailed a gust,
The watchman spied a wreck on The Roaring Bull,
Shot off a Costen light with hurried thrust
And roused his comrades for a long, hard pull
Against a dead head wind and combers brimming full.

Three hours feathering oars against the breeze
They reached the *John P. North,* where eyes looked wide
On their deliverers, though running seas
Foretold a battle with the bucking tide:
Where heaped-up breakers swaggering jealous-eyed
Watched for their chance, the surfboat jockeyed near
The guggling maelstrom at the schooner's side,
And seven tight-lashed men were lowered clear,
While wolf cries on the wind drew ratlines taut with fear.

On lumpy light-green swells they neared the land,
The oars were shipped, the waves made quick retreat;
The men jumped out, and through the scratching sand,
Hauled up the boat, each straining at a cleat:
The seaweed freshly green beneath their feet,
The bonelike driftwood strewn around the dory,
The wind through half-dead trees, the cliffs where beat
Infuriated waves, the fishers hoary,
Portrayed a Spartan scene on a granite promontory.

A door swung, and a woman aproned white
Bade all come in; "We haven't much," she said,
"That's fancy, but we'll try make out a bite
If you can put up with plain fish and bread."
The men devoured the table's ample spread
Of buttered fishcakes, bacon, marmalade;
Kindled their pipes and, snugly billeted,
Lounged in the big front room where birch flames played
Over the braided rug and varnished swordfish blade.

About the stove they sat, safe from the gale,
And told the story of the night before:
How, in the blinding snow they shortened sail,
Seeking the shelter of a harbored shore;
And how, amid the breakers' frightening roar,
The ship misstayed and grated on the reef,
And how they wrote on scantling from the floor
Their names, and pinned them to their coats that grief
Of seekers for the dead might know some slight relief.

Talk drifted back to that unrivaled height
Of terror on the North Atlantic waves—
The gale that struck the *Portland* in the night,
Hurrying all on board to deep-sea graves;
Frozen to rigging, lashed to heavy staves,
Tossed up on rocks where spruces halt the tide,
Men and wrecks on island reefs, in caves,
Bestrewed the coast next morning far and wide—
And pipes went out as each recalled some friend who died.

Another breathless tale that night they told:
How Captain Kidd hove to off the thorn-plum tree,
And sent four men with bars of Spanish gold
In iron chests ashore, but only three
Came back: the fourth was murdered quietly
Beneath the moon; his ghost still wanders there
Annoying treasure-hunters who would free
Those yellow bars from his bleached bones, and dare
Wrest from the pirate's fame dark legends of despair.

These yarns made strong and salt with seacoast phrase
Led up to song: a sailor tried the keys
Of his harmonica in various ways,
And cleaned it out by thumping on his knees;
A ballad-singer feeling quite at ease
Warbled of "John B. Gordon," "Mamie White,"
Bold "Whisky Johnny," and a bracing breeze
Of windlass chanties whose rough notes delight
The men who laugh to scorn the loftier poet's flight.

Twelve quick metallic strokes called loud for sleep;
The crew went out and scanned the pitch-black sky,
Then in soft beds of sheldrake down sank deep,
To dream of wives whom sleep that night passed by:
They heard no more the breakers boiling high,
The pear tree drubbing on the gutter spout,
The rote on distant ledges, or the cry
Of earth—a ship released at one great shout
Scudding her way through space with every reef let out.

Changing Seasons

The wind is full of mystery tonight;
In it the summer warmth and autumn chill
Commingle like the waters in a bight
To form a tide rip that is never still.

Colliding seasons purify the air
Like clouds that forge the thunderbolt; the moon
Treads fearfully her hazy spiral stair,
And clearer grows the laughing of the loon.

When breezes hit them from the bay's defiles,
The little boats at anchor faintly move;
And waves unwind to strike the wooden piles
That eavesdrop too intently on the cove.

The world is full of mystery tonight,
So full that one is satisfied to feel
The wind caress his cheeks, the waves in flight,
The woods withhold the tales they might reveal.

To the Waves

Pound, waves, and beat against the shore;
Lunge along the cliffs, and twist their brown hair
        with your clean white fingers.
Grapple the rocks and rush on.
Scorn their inhuman disdain;
You have the fervor, the sparkle
They need though they notice you not.
When your terrible fury is spent
And peace is pervading your body,
And they reckon you one with themselves—
Pass your silken hands liquidly over their gray,
        indifferent breasts;
Ease your way into their seams,
And liven with motion their silence.
Shock them into submission;
Shock them out of their languor.

Invisible winds push away
At your shoulders; the sea gulls behind you
Clamor antiphonal chorus
To your spray serenading the tree tops.
Time pulls with you as strong
As tides in the spring that forget
The boundaries set for high water,
And gallop like steeds up the coast
Driven full tilt by the moon.
Pound, waves, envelope the shore
Slip in at the headland's brown feet
And curl up like Ruth beside Boaz.

Shore Path

Walking through mossy groves of spruce
When waves thump on a jagged shore,
And tree tops frantically unloose
Air squadrons in a whirring roar,

I hear wave music brokenly,
Hear plaintive calling of the gulls
That touch their wing tips in the sea
Around the schooners' rusty hulls.

Boughs crackle underneath my feet,
A quawk trails long legs overhead,
And orange toadstools bowing greet
My entrance to their springy bed.

The rain has turned the trees' dark green
To pillars of cathedral naves;
And aspergilla boughs between
Sprinkle forgotten Indian graves.

Here in this path of yellow light
The wind and trees and pounding beach
Tear open windows nailed down tight,
And blow all Heaven within my reach.

Morning World

I would not kiss the stupid lips of sleep
And miss the earliest notes of morning birds
Rousing a postlude to the fading stars,
And clamoring for sleepy flowers and herds
To look along the east at every path
And hail the pink sun radiant from his bath.

The bumblebee within the columbine
Polygamously digging at each bell
Stirs moss-rose feelings in my wakening breast

That leave me when the forenoon rays dispel
The facets from the diamonds in the dew,
And ripples from the morning glories' blue.

The drenching fragrances of carraway
And red-top clover from the pastures wind
At rim of dawn, when ducks go wheeling by
To lakes marred only by the hunter's blind;
And distant landscapes lift like fairylands
Changing at noonday into desert sands.

O for an early-morning world to live on;
A world of cool, wine-colored, tree-etched rays
Of dawn light, world of dewy buttercups
And daisies singing white and golden praise
To eastern windows facing apple trees,
And hills baptized in yellow-ocher seas.

Visitor

What I beheld last night how can you know
Who move about among material things?
The ghostly presence of a favoring soul,
Perhaps some gracious lady who abode
Inside these old colonial walls returned.
The white lace on the collar and the sleeves
Of her black gown of watered silk that made
No rustle when she walked; the dignified
Patrician outline of her face against
White paneling where maple boughs and elms
Cast shadows in the moonlight, made her seem
As much at home among us as the trees.
Under the pressure of her gaze I woke,
Whereat she turned away and stood awhile
Beside my first-born's crib, and gently smiled
When he laughed out at something in his dreams.
Then farther off she glided till she came
To baby's cot, and stood there still and long;
Her left hand stretched as if in benediction

100

Over his soft white limbs and rosy face.
The memory of my mother moving round
At night to see if her large brood were safe,
Moving around in darkness quietly—
Relieved what might have been a midnight fear
And led me into fellowship with her
Who peered through deep recesses of the night.

Poet Knowledge

I know the chicadees in early spring
Make wayside firs with bells of Easter ring.

I know the twilight breath of meadow hay
Sprinkles with myrrh the drowsy end of day.

I know the earliest flakes of falling snow
Kindle in me an incandescent glow.

I know, as I go out beneath the stars,
That God himself has taken down the bars

To let me wander in the pastures where
The one impulsive utterance is prayer.

Postlude

The old men along the coast
Are sloopboats of the inner harbor
Lying at their moorings
In peace.
The tide is setting out,
Dragging them all one way,
Their bows looking back toward the shore
Lingeringly,
Longingly.

Night after night
Death, the grim pirate,
A long sharp knife on his bowsprit,
Black sails on his spars,
No starboard or port light showing
Drippingly green or red,
Slips into the harbor
And slashes the hawser
Of one of these sun-blistered craft,
And forth out of sight,
Leaving behind a lonesome, quiet mooring,
It is smuggled forever
Into the limitless, fog-curtained sea.

DOWN EAST

Etching

No more than these: one act, one phrase,
Yet have they haunted all my days.

He wearied into the grocery store,
Slumped by the big stove's open door,

Plucked from the fire a graying coal,
And, trembling it over his briar's bowl,

Lit up, then tossed it in the hod
Sighing despairingly, "My God!"

The calloused finger, calloused thumb
Holding a live coal, struck me dumb;

But deeper callous in his look,
And voice that darkened as it shook,

Made goose flesh on my spirit stand,
With living death so near at hand.

Vigil

Alone on the windy wharf, a Paisley shawl
Drawn tightly down her cheeks, forefingers clutching
Convulsively the folds at her fluttering breast,
The lower corners flapping in the breeze;
Her tear-filled eyes, like the clouds above her head,
Disturbed and moving, strained toward open water,
Watching to see along the blurred horizon
A fishing boat return that rowed away
Early that morning; now, late at night, caught down
To leeward in the equinoctial gale.

Three times their supper had been warmed, and three
Times she had set it on the back of the stove,
While she went out to pace the trembling wharf

And listen for the oars against the tholepins
Above the hissing of the wind-lashed waves—
Listen and strain—while the lines in her face were deepening
Their channels like the cove as she imagined
Their bodies fathoms deep, to be brought in
A fortnight hence so battered that the caskets
Could not be opened in the little parlor.
There loomed also the dark and empty years
Stretching before her, with her other five
To be brought up somehow—God only knew.
Her terror slackened—she heard the tell-tale spank
As the dory's bottom flattened on a wave.
Weary and wet, but loaded to the gunnels
They made the wharf at one; the biggest catch
Of haddock their six trawls had ever swayed to
Lay bulging like gray waves on a wintry sea.

At sight of her the two cried, "Mother, come!"
The son beside himself with eager joy,
The husband sobered somewhat by the storm.
But she, as soon as she beheld them safe,
Collapsed upon the wharf, her vigil over.
The men, amazed, forsook their tying up;
The wind and waves were conquered, but the woman,
Slumped in a pile above her faded shawl
There on the wharf, baffled their seamanship.
They raised her tenderly and led her home,
One on each side, and set her gently down
In the big armchair beside the kitchen stove,
Poured her a cup of tea, and fell asleep,
While she, all night, lay shuddering with the gale.

Captain George

"The sea's my enemy," she kept repeating
Over and over, the night her George was born.
"It washed his father off the *Evelyn's* deck
Three months ago; it carried out and swamped

My brother's boat that took him years to pay for;
My sister's man was frozen to the wheel
The night the *Chase* went down; and now this boy,
Whatever comes, must keep clear of the sea!"

When George was old enough to run away
Out of the yard her law had made his world,
The sable schooners of the coastwide fleet
Voyaging up and down the busy channel
Dropped anchor in his mind. Green wherries deep
With flipping fish stirred something in his blood
That even mother love could not subdue;
But mother love this time was fortified
With years of resolution, and her will
Had grown with that austere decision made
The midnight he was born, until it could
Checkmate and circumvent the slightest move
He made toward the sea.

                    He toiled at play
Like other children, and like others born
In seaport villages battened his mind
On fishing rods and boats of generous color.
Gay toys! but let his mother come upon him
Fondling a boat or reeling up a line
And there would stir a venom in her eyes
That froze the joy in his. One April day,
In town with her, wishing through big glass windows,
His sharp eyes lit upon a tall red sloopboat
And there held fast, until a neighbor seeing,
Beckoned the clerk and whispered, "This for George."
Torn as she was, she let him take it home,
But never once relenting let him see
Or play with it. She kept it in a drawer
Under a lock and key securely hid,
But not secure enough to lock his reverie
That wove dream patterns in and through that craft
Fantastic and alluring as a poet
In idle hours would weave round Spanish galleons
Deep loaded with doubloons.

                                 His fourteenth spring,
Of adolescent whimsies brimming full,
He begged her for a wherry with a sail.
The other boys went racing round the cove,
And on fair days stood out across the harbor,
Wind in their hair and sunlight on their sails,
The buoyant motion of the blossoming waves
Setting them free. Alone on the shore in gloom,
He longed for a boat in vain. This frustrate year
Drawn to its foggy close, he pled to go
To Boston on a lime-coaster that shipped
A neighbor's boy as cook. Rebuffed once more,
He ran off to the city and signed up
To join a battle fleet and see the world.
She guessed his errand through maternal fear
Uncanny and intuitive, made straight
Her journey to the corner of the street,
And so upbraided the recruiting lad
That he gave up the papers, not yet dry.
That afternoon as George walked home his face
Took on a wild and hunted look; he ground
His teeth together as small children do
In great distress of sleep; and all that night
Sleep that had never treated him unkindly
Refused to come. The darkening weeks dragged on,
Autumnal weeks of tossing misery,
His laughter fleeing like red maple leaves
Chased by gray winds. He roamed the shores alone,
Until, before the winter snows had fallen,
An unrelenting winter had closed in
Upon his brain.
                  The turn his mania took
Left him the "Captain" of a full-rigged ship
Pacing the quarter-deck and giving orders:
"Eight bells!" "All hands aloft!" "Come, speak the ship!"
"Keep off, and steer her for the evening star!"
"All hands on deck!" "Furl sail!" "Pay out that hawser!"
"Snub her up short and warp her to the wharf!"
"Keel haul the lazy lout!" "Enough, pipe down!"
Over and over he would keep repeating

Whatever sea terms he had heard or read of
(We wondered where he ever learned so many).
The hungry town fastened upon his plight
To fill its ditty box of anecdote,
Then paid him scant attention till his mother,
Fretful to go at three score years and ten,
Stole down to the wharf one night, untied a boat,
And in delirium put out to sea—
The enemy at last in stranger guise
Than she, or even we, could understand.

When thirty seasons of shell ice had made
Night walking treacherous for nimbler feet,
No longer could he lift the little trees
That fell across his path. Town gossip led
The three selectmen to step in and crown
The careless irony of his existence,
With papers that another George had signed,
By sending him away to Sailor's Snug Harbor.
He shook his head until they talked to him
About the other "Captains" anchored there
In a quiet harbor filled with evening light,
And all sails furled. They saw his eyes flare up,
And, though no word was spoken, knew his gaze
Had rested on bright caravels that still
Were drifting on his mind's Sargasso Sea.
His last day at the shack he worked about
Boarding up windows, puttering with gear,
And banking brush around his old green wherry.
At length he nailed a slab across the door
On which he wrote, "Keep out, I'm coming back."

Islanders going home on lonely nights
Across the harbor past his fallen shack
Say they have seen a light, now green, now red,
Float like a will-o'-the-wisp above his cabin;
Say they have heard a gruff voice on the headland
Call out, "Ahoy!" "Keep off!" or "Whither bound!"
And those to whom they tell the tale go home
Believing silently that George's ghost

Is keeping faith with that crude sign he nailed
Across the door so many years ago.

The Ballad of Poor Annie

Word has come into Galway
That laborers breaking stone
In quarries of the States earn more
Than in Erin was ever known.

"We'll take the Black Ball liner,"
Said Katherine to Tim;
"You work the rock, and I'll keep house;
I've had enough of him."

They took the Black Ball liner
And sailed across the seas;
He blasted rock, and tilled his yard
To the lilt of her melodies.

The green on his potato shoots
Blushed deeper than our own;
And the shine on her pans, the women said,
Must have come from the Blarney stone.

She waxed as fruitful as the soil—
Her first a buxom boy,
Christened for the Galway lad
Had crowned herself with joy.

Word has come into Galway
That Katherine was seen
By an Irish tar who loudly swore
Her grace would vex a queen.

One August morning when the sun
Poured down on cove and bay
A weather-breeding lustre, long
She watched her boy at play,

And felt the first leap of a babe,
Would join him on the floor,
When looking up she saw a form
Walk slowly toward the door.

"Mavrone! Mavrone!" cried Katherine,
"So you have come at last—
The only creature on this earth
My happiness could blast.

"You were the black ball in that sail
Above us on the sea—
The one black spot on my white flesh
Would stain the life of me."

He stood, nor answered her a word;
She swooned across the sill;
He raised her up—then turned away;
The sultry air grew chill.

The curse of God was in that turn;
Or was he Satan's tool?
Young Annie, born on New Year's day,
Became the village fool.

Some in the village still believe
Her husband never came—
Believe Kate saw a phantom grow
From shadows in her brain

When she was four months into child;
But others say he walked
Along the stone sheds, wan and wild
As to himself he talked.

The cottage by the cove is gone;
Gone Tim and blue-eyed Kate;
Poor Annie gibbers on the street
From early unto late

Of berries she has picked to sell,
Of someone she will wed:
And the town will bury birthmark fears
When her last mass is said.

Incident of the Coast

One cold December morning—crackling cold,
The metal waters of Penobscot Bay
Curled into vapor on the zero air,
When Harry, rising from his bed to haul,
Said, "Brrr, it's bitter, bet my mittens freeze
Stiff between each pot out there in the bay."

His young wife, starting coffee, begged in vain,
"Harry, leave your boat stay on the mooring."

Into the cold he went: he heard a board
Burst from a nail on the barn as he went by;
He felt a hardness in the path that met
His rubber boots with stubborn enmity;
He saw a poplar shivering in the air
Where no wind was; dragged, over delicate ice,
His tender to the motorboat; far off
Saw vapor rising like a pillar of cloud
Over the bay; then, hesitant, stooped down,
Turned on his gas, drained twice his priming cup,
Spun round and round the wheel, and left the cove.
An hour's run, he made his outmost trap,
And gaffed the buoy, floating white and red,
The red sparkling with frost, the white lit up
With ruddy streaks out of the eastern sky,
As sunrise flaming through the cold air turned
The bay to a crater bright enough to catch
Indifferent eyes and hold them with its roll
And flow of streaming wine-drip over the sea.

In his eyes no indifference: he saw
Too well the play of tint on tint, awe-struck

At all the panorama of the morning:
Ultramarine above, gun-barrel blue
Along the bleak horizon, while around
The red cliffs of the islands weird mirages
Blurred the fixed lines of distance over the bay
Till they went antigodling everywhere,
Like northern lights across an Arctic sky.
Mechanically he took the counters out,
Baited his trap, and, heedless, threw it over,
His mind preoccupied with loveliness;
Started his engine dreamily, then woke
To find the tangled warp had twisted round
The whirling shaft and blades of his propeller,
So tightly drawn the flywheel would not budge.

White scuds were rising in the northwest now,
A breeze was ruffling green and white the bay.
He felt the woolen mittens on his hands
Stiffen with ice; alarmingly he felt
His body stiffen, and lean hounds of cold
With snapping teeth jab at his whitened skin.
"I'm going for it," he cried out, recalling
Long-forgotten tales of freezing men.
Desperate, he grabbed a cod line, threw it over,
Relayed it in, and threw it out again,
Till eighty times had set his young blood stirring.
His hands grew warm, his mittens limp. He tried
Pulling the warp out with his gaff, but made
No headway—and the north wind piping on.

Death tightened on that warp and challenged him.
He knew no rescue boat would come; he heard
Death's mockery snarling on the icy wind,
And met the challenge. Stripping off his clothes,
Stark naked, with a splitting knife in hand,
He plunged in the wintry waters, swimming down
Under the stern, where he slashed and pulled away
The deadly warp, till, at the last frayed end
Of the warp that bound him to the trap of life,
He tumbled over the side, teeth chattering, numb,
Hauled on his clothes, and headed for the harbor.

Down to the ice-caked shore the neighbors came,
Watching his wherry push the waves apart.
Laden with layers of ice, caught from the spray
And held in all its dazzling glitter fast
Upon the washboards, low on the waves she sagged;
And when he pulled his switch, men clambered down,
Steadied his feet, faltering on frozen seaweed,
And moored his craft, while he went stumbling home.

Miracle

What Providence had singled out our cove
On this November night we never knew:
The fact was there—for there her black hulk lay
Fast in the mud after the wildest night
Our coast had ever known—a lubberly two-master
That should have been condemned ten years before
Surviving—while the stoutest had gone down
With scores of sailors frozen in the shrouds.

His crew went home next morning, but the Captain
Hung round the village waiting for a tug
Two blustering weeks, and every evening told
The tale of that November hurricane,
And his part in the *Lida B.* that night.

We followed him like true believers hearing
The breathless story of a miracle—
For nothing but a miracle, we said,
Could 'a' kept her off the honeycomb of ledges
That studded all the region to the north
Of where she lay, for nearly fifteen miles:
Unbuoyed ledges, half-tide sunken ledges,
And treacherous island reefs at every turn.

"From Blue Hill Bay to this mud cove down here
I didn't know where I was more'n half the time.
I knew the wind was veering round northeast,
But didn't think much of it till the snow

114

Began to spit, the wind to freshen on.
'Let's put her in,' said I, 'to Rockland Harbor,
And lay behind the breakwater all night.'
But long before we made the breakwater
The snow was blinding us. It blowed so hard
We reefed the mainsail, took the foresail down,
And steadied her a little with the jib.
Pretty soon the sea broke over the stern
And we just ran before it under bare poles.
When night closed down, I thought, 'I'll run her on
To any beach we find.' We picked up one;
I know now 'twas Ash Point we blundered into.
I rammed her on, grabbed up my shooting iron
And fired all the cartridges I had,
Thinking the village might rouse up and help us.
But not a soul came down, or if they did
They came too late. Our hooker wouldn't stick,
So I hermed up the wheel and payed her off,
Letting her go hell-bent before the wind.
From Ash Point here was just one sheet of white;
We hadn't been five minutes off when I saw
Big breakers rolling up on the starboard side,
Then looked to port and saw them just as high.
I thought I must be seeing things—called John,
Said I, 'For God's sake, John, can them be breakers?'
And he, 'Yes, father, that's just what they are.'
Well, that's the way it was from there to here:
I've looked at Eldridge' chart till now it's dirty,
And asked myself how in the name of God
I ever squeezed that hulk between them ledges.
There ain't no answer, unless, perhaps, it's this:
A man will die when his time comes—not until."

Whistling Buoy

The whistling buoy off our coast that warns,
"Beware the reef, beware the reef close by!"
Had so laid hold on my quick sympathy
That I had pictured it as truly human,

A new Prometheus, starved of comradeship,
Befriending man against the elements,
Chained in exile on a desolate ocean.

Then one October evening when the calm
Of early autumn had subdued the harbor,
We drifted out to sea for all-night hakeing.
The quietude that brooded on the shore
Had not spread out its wing tips over the bay;
A groundswell raked the bottom of the channel,
And, though the wind was still, the rolling waves
Kept our pinky's wrought-iron traveller hard at work
As the mainsail fretted and shook from side to side.

That night we put down anchor scarcely more
Than fifty yards away from the whistling buoy,
Which all night long kept up its dolorous groan
Continually in a jerky rise and fall,
Laying its round black length across a wave
Whenever the undertow scooped out a hollow
Beneath its mooring. Hour on hour I watched
It lunge and plunge in the pyramidal swell,
Writhing like a great sperm whale between
The time a harpoon hits him and he dies.
And as the night birds flew around our boat,
With cries as boding as the dismal buoy,
The sympathy that wakened long before
Died in me, and this towering shape became
The unheeding and inexorable god
Of "infinite eternal energy,"
Spawn of a mechanistic century—
A god when found was scarcely worth the finding,
Indifferent, impersonal, alone.

An Indiana Pioneer

A long poke bonnet, limp earth-colored dress,
And spectacles with tarnished silver rims
Reposing on a splendid Roman nose,

116

Could not conceal the blue quicksilver eyes
That smiled as if to twinkle "howdy-do"
In friendly Hoosier greeting. She saw at once
I loved her blossoming old-fashioned garden,
And asked if I would like to mosey through.

This visit spurred my appetite to know
What roots lay hid beneath the roots she tended;
So Sunday after Sunday I drew up
By her log cabin; and one afternoon
When skies were more expansive than before,
And purple haze more gently brushed the hills,
She blossomed into speech and told me how
She came to cast her lot among the flowers.

"For years I wanted pretty things at home,
Nice furniture, wallpaper, curtains, books,
And great big plate-glass winders facin' south.
(The Bible mentions *chambers of the south,*
And I have loved that passage all my life.)
But John was close, and hated all my plans,
Puttin' me off till Victor's letter come
Out of the Klondike. I was so set up
I clean forgot that night to feed the hens.

'Now, mother, buy you what you want,' he wrote;
So then and there I started fixin' up
By fetchin' first of all an easy chair—
I thought he'd find it nice to set and smoke in.
When he come in, he looked at it askew,
Then turned on me, his face a ragin' bull's,
Snarlin', 'Now, Mary, if you carry here
Another of your fancy thingumbobs,
I'll take this axe' (he clenched it till his knuckles
Were whiter than them sheets there on the line)
'And smash your doodads to a thousand pieces.'

"For nights I laid awake and tossed and turned,
Starin' and wonderin' how I might work out
Some way to slake my thirst for pretty things;
And finally without a word I quit

Truck-gardenin', and raisin' geese and hens,
And made a bed of amaryllis, phlox,
Laburnum, buttercups, and marigolds,
Gardenias, sweet william, columbine,
And all the roses in the catalogue;
And as I planned my garden in the night
The flowers seemed sproutin' down inside my dreams,
And come up better for the dirt my mind
Had had heaped on it for a dozen years.
And first he used to come around and nag
Sayin' this posy bed was foolishness,
Would bring no ready money for the house;
And then again he'd grow more lovin'-like
And say I was the flower in the garden
He liked the best, and other such-like blarney.
But nothin' he could say would alter me;
So on I worked and puttered half the night,
And dreamed about my flowers the other half
Till here is what you see." Her face lit up
When she stretched out her hand, as if a light
Quite hid from me were shining on the petals.

The Ballad of Jonathan Coe

'Twas on a cloudless first of June
In Hampstead years ago,
Two daughters, out at work, came home
To the farm of Jonathan Coe.

They came on Saturday afternoon,
With Congress shoes for him;
Their own hearts set on wearing next day
Bright silks and ribbons trim.

Mary, the elder, at supper said,
"When we all go up to our pews
Will you humor us for just this once
By wearing these brand-new shoes?"

118

"We will go to church as we always did
When ye lived at home with us;
And as for my feet, I would have them shod
In the sandals of righteousness."

Alone in their chamber at nine o'clock,
Combing and curling their hair,
They thought, "Tomorrow we two will be
The envy of Hampstead's fair."

When next the clock struck nine he rose
And stood like Jephthah strong—
The black-bound Book in his massive hand,
His black beard rough and long,
But never a shoe, or old or new,
Would he wear in the godly throng.

Barefoot, he strode that mile to church;
His daughters, still as stone,
On each side keeping pace with him
Checked many an inward groan.

Children running on ahead
Had spread the news before,
And when he reached the church a crowd,
Foregathered at the door,

Stared at his face set hard as flint
Against vainglorious Pride;
He sat down in the second pew,
A daughter on each side,
And everyone in Hampstead knew
How they were mortified.

His Martha never cast again
Her shadow on his door;
And the light that shone in Mary's face
Dimmed from that very hour.

But the Lord God won a victory
Through Jonathan, His light,

As God, through Jephthah, won of old
Against the Ammonite;
So let us laud and magnify
In song His wondrous might!

The Leather Man

The century that tossed upon our shores
The driftwood of a continent, dispersed
Among the salvageable timber bits
That would not fill our rocky crevices,
Or burrow in our ever shifting sand
Until the blown sand of oblivion
Should cover them forever. One of these
Misfits of human flotsam tossed about
The hills and valleys of Connecticut,
Took root in minds starved of romance and grew
To be the legend of the Leather Man.

Thin was the basis of the tale: men saw
A creature wandering from town to town
Clad all in leather: boots, cap, trousers, shirt,
A leather pouch with strap and leather buckles
Over his shoulders. Keener eyes saw more,
For this man's eyes, brown as his vestment, clear
As sandspring water on October dawns,
Held in their depths a fathomless retreat.

The legend grew when he refused with thanks
Mercies from hands not vibrant with his own;
Or charmed the children like the Hamelin piper—
His pipe the lore of beasts and flowers told
In English accents tinged with Gallic stress.
His quaintly spoken, "Children, gather round
And hear a tale the laurel told to me
As I was lying on the Cornwall hills";
Or "Hear this lion story," as he flashed
A burnished jewel out of La Fontaine,
Set him apart from all the wandering tribe.

120

Over the hills he went from town to town,
No money in his purse, no second suit,
Like some belated follower of him
Who made Assisi famous, or of One,
In days far more remote, who entertained
Small children in the towns of Galilee.
He grew familiar to the countryside,
If such a shadowy figure ever could
Be called familiar. Once a year he made
The circuit of the state: now following
The river towns from Lyme to Windsor Locks;
Now in the Berkshire foothills, sleeping out
Near Cornwall, Sharon, Torrington, or Kent;
Now on the Sound, from Stamford to Noank.

The spring in certain towns was marked for years
By his appearance, and in these he walked
As welcome as a messenger from Heaven.
When children cried, "Here comes the Leather Man!"
The farmers mused, " 'T is time to plough"; their wives,
" 'T is time to turn the carpets"; everywhere
The children met him on the village green
To hear his tales of animals, and see
A creature different from the homespun folk
They walked and talked with fifty weeks a year.

About him songs sprang up; such verses as,
"O Mister Leather Man, tell us your story,"
Linger among us yet. About him, too,
There drifted in weird tales from overseas
Of his long-buried life. The favorite,
That wove a spell like mist upon these hills
In which mild antiquarians dipped their pens,
Needs little of a poet's broidery.

In youth he drank the wines of Burgundy;
And like his father in a tannery spent
Long hours beside the fleshing post until
One afternoon at twilight hurrying home
He, like the Florentine, beheld a maiden
Clad all in red, and straightway fell in love

As only those can fall who ponder long
And lovingly on beauty. She, in turn,
Feasting her eyes of April blue on his
Autumnal eyes of brown, and entering
His shadowy glades of otherworldliness,
Vowed through the coming seasons she would wed
Her beauty to his dreams. Her father laughed
The day his wife revealed their youthful love;
Sole owner of the tannery, he nursed
Far larger plans for her. But when she grew
Unswerving in her course, his acid flings
Gave way to threatening denunciations
That failed to loose her purpose from its moorings.
Devotion such as this, like sparkling waves
Beating on granite and reshaping it
To lines less angular, prevailed at last
Upon the maiden's father—glowering looks
Gave way to smiles, the boy was ushered in
(Though not without misgivings on the part
Of one who knew but vaguely his own shop)
And told of his acceptance as a son,
To be the foreman of the tannery.

Ineptitude had played a winning card
In making this man boss of other men;
No thought of distribution, output, cost,
Had ever vexed him—he had worked content,
Or numbed his discontent, beside the beam
His father labored at for forty years.
If more than this crept in to challenge him
It lay beyond the tannery walls; to know
The lore of flowers, or the hardier blooms
Of poetry, to his estate denied.
His first thought was, "I must begin to fill
This dark and empty hold with merchandise
Of East and West—the culture of the world
It long has waited for." The pilot chosen
To guide him to this treasure trove first steered
Him through the syntax of the Gallic Wars.
The suicide of bold Orgetorix
Troubled him not a little, but the fights

And bridges built across the Rhine were lost
On one whose mind was by the bridge that links
Fond heart to heart. Haranguing Cicero
Fared little better; but the Mantuan,
With Dido and the voyages by sea,
And darker voyage to the nether world,
Endeared him to the classics as he stood
Half willing to let ship and cargo drown.

While he fared thus in search of classic lore,
The tannery was left to drift along
Without a guiding hand. His workmen loafed,
Gathering discontent as ships in port
Grow barnacles and eelgrass on their hulls.
The foremen of his rival tanneries
Won over his skilled workers, hardened souls
Still rankling at the fate that touched a pawn
And fashioned it a knight. The incompetent
Wailed to the town their petty woes and stayed,
But not for long; before the round full moon
Had flooded thirty times their chamber windows,
The tannery with all its prestige failed.
Meanwhile his wife, a flower unfit to bide
The lashing gales of censure that increased
With every passing month, drooped on the stem
And wilted to the ground. His hope went out,
And like the sea in Virgil's nether world
Despair came rushing turbulently through him;
Bewildered, overwhelmed with grief, intent,
Like bold Orgetorix, on suicide,
But stayed by unseen forces, he escaped
In great confusion to the coast, and shipped
On board a clipper for the Western world.

Remorse that comes and goes in normal men,
Cast out by new resolves or fresh employ,
In this man grew to be a shrine at which
He worshipped, as Saint Francis whom he loved
Made vows to Poverty; the outward sign
Of his Remorse the brown investiture
That shrivelled him to ruin and brought down

Upon his house, his loved one's hearth and hopes,
The pillars holding up their little Gaza.
As penance for his sin he clad himself
From head to foot in leather and set out
Upon his wanderings—thinking to atone,
Far as atonement could be made, for all
The grief he wrought, by keeping day and night
Before his mind the instrument of woe
His blundering had wielded. In his head
High snatches of great poetry remained
To soften his remorse; and in these hills,
These laureled hills that hold so much of beauty—
A lodestone ever tugging at his heart—
He gave himself to endless wandering.
So here beneath this sky he passed his days,
And built unwittingly his eerie legend,
Until one night, one stormy winter's night,
Under a cave near Bristol he lay down,
And when the morning dawned his leather case
Became his casket and memorial.

January Thaw

Noon, and the tall black trees
That lean on the frozen river
Shed drops too mild to freeze,
Though the sun seems gone forever.

Elm tops melt in the mist,
The gray-white mist that throws
A mantle of amethyst
As far as the skyline goes,

A melting that helps to trace
On patches of smooth blue ice
Contours of motley grace
In the roadbed's fall and rise;

Contours I will not break,
But will drive far out around,
That beauty may not forsake
This cold, hard ground.

Wave Music

Behind this bowlder on the shore,
After a night of wind and rain,
I lie and let the waves restore
The jaded tissues of my brain.
Why can no inland mountain strain
So flood with ecstasy my flesh?
No inland waters float a seine
To snare my fancy in its mesh?

There is an undertow in me
That only moves when some great gale
Kicks up an undertow at sea,
Starting an orchestra going full scale:
Woodwinds full toned, and strings assail
High cliffs in bristling undismay:
Beneath, loud drums and brasses flail
Dark ledges hidden in the bay.

There may be in an island birth
A need unknown to inland men—
Need for an armistice with earth
To let salt tides flow in again.
"Dust to dust" was spoken when
The race had not yet found the sea;
A deeper call has come since then—
"Salt brine to blood," for men like me.

Heritage

They made their graveyards on the hill,
Their houses just below,
And something from the tombs came down
The slope long years ago;

It fastened on the cellar walls,
It climbed the rough-hewn beams
Clear to the attic, back again,
And mildewed in the seams—

Till those who called these dwellings home
Saw the dark spate leave behind
A tiny fringe of graveyard loam
Upon New England's mind.

Wolf

Behind my house a timber wolf
Prowls almost every day;
I fear him, for he wants to snatch
My wistful hound away;
She loves to watch his quiet tread,
His muscles' sinewy play.

Twice have I come home suddenly
And found him near the gate.
One glance, and his receding back
Loped off at such a rate
I could only see his tracks in snow,
And a streak that flashed like hate.

My wistful hound looks up at me
And knows my heart is wrung,
Knows well my cup of sleep is drained
By his too thirsty tongue—
Yet she yearns and burns to follow him
And litter his den with young.

Stay Back, Age

Stay back up the hill, Age, stay back,
Be patient at finding my will
Alert for new paths of adventure
This side of the hill:

For the regions I care to explore
Lie east of the rim;
Let me ruminate here a while longer;
Let me revel and swim

In the meadows and rivers all summer—
O summer, be long!
Come autumn, I'll join, though protesting,
The circumspect throng.

I know the last rise will be hardest,
I shall toil out of breath,
And the shouts of the younglings behind me
Will pierce me like death.

Stay back, let me make it without you,
Overtake you beyond the divide,
Well down, may it be, from the summit
Where breezes have died.

Spruces

Let us study how spruces grow old:
The texture of bark, and the rings
In the grain, and the straightness that sings.

I remember how soldiers grew old
Who had slept out four years under trees,
And behold, they had caught in the breeze

A hint—they were stalwart and straight,
Tanned deep as spruce bark in the sun;
A hint? They had caught more than one

Sleeping out under trees in the cold,
Long branches set off by the stars,
Like their flags—and perhaps a few bars,

In a measure the world had forgot,
Drifting down from the boughs had imbued
Their blood with the surge of the wood.

Let us study how spruces grow old,
And learn, as the balsam runs dry,
To thrust a top limb to the sky.

Hillside Trees

Black trees against a marble hill
Of January snow declare
New England to whoever will
Behold them darkly standing there.

Despoiled of leaves, uncheered by sun
Save now and then a grudging dole,
They stand like berserks every one,
Denied the berserks' wassail bowl.

On days less friendly to the dark,
Chastened, they climb the little rise,
And lift slim hands in prayer to mark
Their kinship with ascetic skies—

A kinship whose serene repose
On mornings after snow has blown
Dwells deepest on the branch that throws
Blue shadows over walls of stone.

128

Clinging Vine

The waters move about these rocks
So softly one would almost guess
The hard gray granite might relent
And mellow at such wantonness.

The mosses on these ledges lie
So pliantly we calculate
The wood's most yielding moss prefers
The roughest bowlder for a mate.

Wherefore should not the lovely lass,
Tender as pussy-willow boughs,
Shyer than dew on sunlit grass,
Cleave to the adamantine spouse?

Zeb Kinney on Feminism

"I tell you, broody hens don't lay no eggs.
You girls can talk till doomsday tellin' me
About the things you want to paint and write—
But all the time they's something on your mind.
It ain't the same with Waugh and Dougherty:
Let Waugh get started any afternoon
When they's an undertow a-runnin' strong
Enough to make the ocean buckle under—
And I don't s'pose the most upstandin' girl
That rusticates round here could make him budge.
But you girls stand with one eye on your paintin',
The other on the fellers passin' by,
A-sayin' to yourself, 'I wonder who
That youngster might be standin' over there;
I wonder if that older one is married.'
That's why your pictures ain't like Waugh's and
        Dougherty's—
Their waves is waves, but yours is sort o' mongrel—
Half waves and half a longin' for the fellers.
I tell you, broody hens don't lay no eggs."

Concarneau

At medieval Concarneau
The small black luggers come and go
Round headlands dear to fishermen
Burnished today as cliffs were when
The Druid altars near the sea
Crowned tawny hills of Brittany.

The crier's bell and lusty calls
Awaken us to streets and stalls
Where wooden shoes on cobblestones
Go clattering still their ancient tones;
Where Breton caps charm passers-by
Like white-lace clouds against blue sky;
Where girls in sardine factories singing,
Bright-eyed and buxom, match the ringing
Carousal songs in blithe buvettes
Of Breton boys; where sea-blue nets
Like sapphire rings out on display
Brighten the fingers of the bay.

The old gray fort, with moss-green sides
And one gray church to mark the tides
Of spirit, broods above a stream
Yielding itself to many a dream
Of years when Danish pirates came
To fight for fishing lands and fame.

Below the fort's now tumbling wall
Bright sails reflect the sunset's fall;
The big fleet on the harbor lies
Like iridescent butterflies
Together huddled on soft down
With wings of yellow, blue, and brown;
Or like a great rose window flaming
In some twelfth-century nave proclaiming
Zeal of a race whose rose of art
Unfolded from a flaming heart.

When gray days chill New England's glow,
I dream your colors, Concarneau.

130

Coast Cathedral

Alone on the cliff. Below me fathoms deep
Come echoes tumbling out of ocean caves
Whose overtones arouse me like the leap
Of *Sursum corda* high in Gothic naves.

Alone, and yet the scent of bayberry leaves,
Mingled with briny savor, floods the air
With incense which my weariness receives
Like hyssop drifting from an altar stair.

How can I feel alone when great clouds run
Out of the north and poise above the sea,
Flanking the bright rose window of the sun
With blue-white panels of immensity?

A gliding gull descending from the sky,
An unexpected porpoise puffing near,
A gray-black harbor seal, nose lifted high,
Saint Francis might call brothers were he here.

And he would know that symbols others find
In vast cathedrals flowering out of Rome
To minister to something more than mind,
Emerge where dark cliffs kneel in ocean foam.

Morning Walk

This path that leads me to the cove
Is lambrequinned with greenest moss
On which dim lights and shadows rove
Unhurriedly where dark boughs cross.

A squirrel at his morning meal
Sits up and greets me on my walk
As children greet when strangers feel
Impelled to draw them into talk.

Gay toadstools, lavender and red,
A shoal of mushrooms turning brown,
And chickadees, long out of bed,
Salute me as I saunter down.

And when, too soon, I reach the end
And come upon the open sea,
The morning sun swims round the bend
And dazzlingly embraces me.

Sea Song

This land is the pride of its owner,
But no one holds in fee
The flowing tides that wander
In and out of the sea.

The fruits of the land lie tethered,
But the graceful yield of the sea
Purples green caves with shadows
That shuttle elusively.

No storm through a notch in the mountains
Unrolls such pageantry
As breakers leaping toward ragged clouds
From a reef in a northern sea.

No calm of fields at twilight
Mirrors placidity
With quite the languid rondure
Of still tides under a lee.

For the high course of adventure
To the regions of the free
The restless take their bearings
By the restless, restful sea.

Fog

Soothe me, O fog, till I can keep as still
As fishing boats at anchor in this bight
That scarcely tug against the slow tide's will
Enough to fetch their mooring-painters tight.

Hide me, O fog, till I can quite shut out
The claims and clamors of the distant town—
Can know myself and what I am about
Before the ebb tide lays the rockweed down.

Give me, O fog, of your astringent dew,
Nor spare the dark drop at its crystal base,
Till I, like Mithridates at his brew,
Can drink without once puckering my face.

Address to a Thicket

Tinselled spruces, huddled here
Together where few sunbeams play,
If you could keep your spaces clear,
Nor twine your roots in others' clay,
These lower limbs of yours would hold
Their bloom, and when the sun came out
On evergreen, its shower of gold,
Blood-warm, would girdle you about
As now it girds these taller four
Standing apart above the shore.

Silent spruces, this deep gloom,
Cathedral-like, you linger through,
Is musty as a Valois tomb;
We feel its hush as pilgrims do
On entering a shrine; are stilled
With awe slow pacing up your aisle
Of moss where no sound falls; are filled
With thoughts of "Holy, Holy," while

A thrush note rising clear and free
Thrills like a glad doxology.

Be not deluded: Death decrees
Upon this altar as the priest
The old Druidic mysteries;
The lichened limb has not yet ceased
Its ancient rite; your branches fall
And lie among the mosses dead;
Your trunks, on which gray spiders crawl,
Are stunted, and your taproots fed
On their own substance fallen away,
Fast crumbling to a soft decay.

Ponder the strength of those who shun
The clump, who root where tempests roar
Out of the ocean: wind and sun
Roll in on them till they no more
Need cower under gusts of rain;
The moisture clinging to their boughs
Pours vigor into every vein
Till they are mansions fit to house
Fish hawks and eagles whose high bowers
Look down on village belfry towers.

Secret

You are keeping something from me, Mother Earth;
I have heard the wind consulting with the trees:
"Shall we tell it? He is anxious. Is it worth
Our while to keep it dark from such as these?"

You are keeping something from me; I have seen
A shadow on the water move and stand,
Then disappear where darkness left the green—
And have gone to look for traces on the sand.

You are keeping something from me that the moon
Almost compels you to reveal in spring

134

When one glint more would pluck from you the tune
Judean shepherds heard the angels sing.

On summer dawns you half-decide to tell:
The sun, advancing with deceitful rays,
Declares the hour has come to break the spell,
And still you tantalize me with delays.

Were I a dark Chaldean who could read
The hieroglyphics of the midnight spheres,
I then might know what just escapes my heed
In this persisting shadow of the years.

There Yet Remain

Apple trees slouching down hill,
Gnarled and dry,
Sprawl as neglected as the water mill
Rotting hard by.

In their shade leans a farmhouse, once white,
Roof-sunken, green blinds among roses—
The windowpanes chromed with a light
Time and time only discloses.

By a window the face of a saint
Heeds no more the world's cry—
The world undetecting the faint
Afterglow in her eye.

Sea Garden

The moon is a yellow sunflower
Rising out of a meadow of mold,
Climbing up fences of island and reef,
Looking into a garden of gold.

In the first cool tinge of the evening,
When sea fragrance gathers new zest,
Out of the east, rising big as a sun,
It reaches far into the west—

Showing borders of billowy sweetgrass,
Dotted with bulbs of old rocks,
Alive with jewelweed fishes
That dart out from under green docks;

Sprinkled with drops from the Dipper,
Harrowed with winds from the sky—
A garden as blooming on midwinter nights
As gardens on shore in July.

De Profundis

Out of the waters of defeat unfold
From blackest bogs the lilies' white and gold.

Out of the *rigor mortis* of despair
The leaden features win a marble air.

Out of a crushed and beaten soul young shoots
Break forth, like buds from desiccated roots.

The lotus flower on which the Buddha sits
Springs from the ooze and slime of muddy pits.

The Storm

Ever sounding, falling, pounding
On the ledges of the shore,
Swirling over rocks and curling,
Hurling spray against my door—
Waves, wide-scattering, lunge in, spattering
Brine on fields that shrink to sup

136

The foaming flagons of green dragons
That would eat the headland up.

Watch and listen! whitecaps glisten,
Tide at midnight sweeps the land,
Lifting wreckage that goes drifting,
Sifting pebbles into sand—
Sand, upwinging, showers the singing
Trees that vibrate with the sound
Of waves tumbling, groaning, rumbling
In rock caverns underground.

What mad whirring in earth stirring
Shatters crystals in my brain,
Tears me wide apart, nor spares me,
Bears me back to youth again?
I go soaring with the roaring
Of the elements enraged;
And a part of me falls dormant
When the tempest is assuaged.

And Must I Say Farewell
(To Jeannette)

And must I say farewell
To mornings such as these when crystal air
Flavors the earth as salt flavors the sea;
When sunlight warms the giant monoliths
On which men love to ruminate like seals,
Lost to the petty worries of the town?
And must I never hear
Again the snowy-breasted gulls call out
Their clamor to the shore; or laughing gull
Ha! Ha! his mock derision to the tide?
And never, never feed
My eyes again on shadows from white sails
Quivering near birch-tree shadows by the shore;
Or watch the rockweed float on tawny ledges,
Lullabying periwinkles at half-tide?

And must I say farewell
To you, more precious than the morning sunlight,
More tender than the mist on summer ocean,
More permanent than granite to my need?
Should I go first across the oozy channel,
In quiet seasons I will come to you,
Will come at midnight when the bay's soft silver
Is cleft with one wide lane of quivering gold—
Come to you sleeping when Orion reaches
The crowded summit of his glittering hill,
And crowd your mind with youth's long memories:
Impart my spirit's breathing to your hair,
Let my blood beat again in tune with yours,
My eyes meet your sea-troubled eyes once more;
Then will you wake
To know your dream was something more than dream,
Aware Love's flame reached out across the void,
And over your planet's darkness lit the stars.

Morning by the Sea

Give me the morning on Penobscot Bay—
At daybreak when the sun's returning force
Is drying off the rocks whose colors play
More richly in the moisture; let the course
Of tides be low in order that the weirs
May cast their deepest shadows on the sea,
And the ebon rock that almost never rears
His length hold tired shags upon his knee.
And let it be the morning after rain
And fog and storm have bullied us a week—
The glad note in the gulls is here again,
The driftwood on the shore is new; waves speak
The madness they have revelled in: each one,
Breaking upon the beach, shouts to the sun.

Workers in Stone

Workers in stone, we will not be upset
At all the changing flurries of the time;
This syenite has chosen to forget
That it was molten once, and in its prime
Roved here and there the gray primordial slime
As restless as a mammal in a cage;
Then doubting there were lovelier zones to climb
It here protestingly accepted age.
We've trodden it as actors tread a stage,
We've driven it with bolts to hold our skiffs;
Our doorsteps, hearthstones, headstones—each a page
Of our own Bible, quarried out of cliffs.
Its grain has entered in our very marrows
Till we can blunt the heads of poisoned arrows.

A Maine Winter's Night

The earth, in frozen drapery of snow,
On which the great stars delicately light,
Is quiet as the Milky Way whose bright
Uneven pennons match Orion's glow;
The brooklets trickling on their wintry flow
In muted monotone, hurry their flight
Close by the ocean whose patrols at night
Boom deep with dark December's undertow.

O winter night on cold Penobscot Bay,
Your crystal stars through crystal air appear
Transfigured like the tall brown cliffs that stand
By waiting groves of spruce to watch the play
Of shadows on dark waters hovering near,
Bringing full nets of beauty to the land.

November Cornfield

The tattered standards of the broken corn
Rustle defiance on the frozen blast
Prowling to wreck them; blouses now outworn
That gave their youth a gay mid-April cast
When on parade, cover today instead
A decimated legion old and proud—
Their dry bones rattle in the breeze; their bed,
Ice-cold at night, awaits the long white shroud.

A canteen hanging loosely here and there
For rats and crows to riddle, grim and tall
They stand and look across the low stone wall
At larch and bayberry as fresh and fair
As they when first they sprang up on the field
And took their general orders not to yield.

Clean as These Rocks

Clean as these rocks are, washed by every tide,
Sweet as the fragrance of the summer sea,
Sparkling as sunlight on the waves, and wide
As ocean I would wish my life to be.
Others may feel the rocks too self-contained,
The fragrance lost in pockets up the bay,
The dazzling sun on waves too unrestrained,
Too chilling ocean's battery of spray.

For me these granite barricades suffice
To beat back waves of unrest one by one;
The heady tang of brine holds Orient spice
Tinctured with ambergris; each dart of sun
On waves is foe to dullness; and the ocean
A slug horn call to deepen my emotion.

Groundswell

Often at midnight I have left my bed,
Opened the kitchen door, not knowing why,
And stepped out in the yard whose silence shed
No balm on my unrest; turned to the sky,
Star-poised, in quiet league with elm and oak,
Whose overshadowing calm confounded me;
Slowly the reason for my coming broke—
I heard far off the motion of the sea.

Dead the whole belt of calms; my spirit craved
In those volcanic crises vastly more;
The rote on distant shoals, resounding, saved,
When harbors muffled by an inland shore
Were mockeries; deep registered to deep,
Filling a need beyond all need of sleep.

Invitation to Connecticut
(To I. V. D.)

The pear and plum trees stand in wait for you
Who love their whiteness; underneath their limbs
The robins cock their heads and hearken through
The sod for earthworms stirring; round the rims
Of little hollows red-bud maples fling
Gay streamers beckoning, "Kindle here your fire;
Broil well your steak, forget your cares, and sing,
And yield the savage in you his desire."

Over the coffee we shall hold long talk,
And for you I will pluck the valley's best
Pink lady-slippers; homeward let us walk
While beaten gold is minting in the west;
And I can promise, if you keep quite still,
Beside the brook, a glorious whippoorwill.

Clearing Off

The birds sing "Clearing off," hopping about
And rousing us with merrymaking cheer;
Into the west the wind begins to veer,
Baffling a while, then brandishing to rout
The forces of the east whose last redoubt
Surrenders as the vapors disappear
Above the fog; brigades of blue strike fear
In torn gray flanks till no cloud ventures out.
Within the woods the raindrops scatter and drip
As if tall spruces heeded not the sky.
Because their trunks are fastened in the grip
Of boggy earth, do trees forever cry
For a dark to match their roots? In answer fall
The drip-drop, drip-drop, spattering over all.

Tide Cycle

I. HIGH TIDE

You are different every morning, rocky shore—
Today the full flood tide comes welling through
Each crevice of each bowlder at my door,
And, risen level with the meadow rue,
Jewelweed, purple asters, wild sweet peas,
And morning-glories bordering the bank,
Coaxes the driftwood tossed by windy seas
To shove out here and there a needed plank
And bridge the gap between the sea and land—
Uplifted by your slow rise I am caught
Twice over when a seagull takes his stand—
Illumined whiteness in a rounded spot
Upon a ruddy ledge, as if the full
Flood tide of life were brimming in a gull.

II. LOW TIDE

You are different every morning, rocky shore—
Today the tide has gone and left you bare;
But did not leave until the robes she wore
Were wrapped around her little ones with care.
The cloak of eelgrass, winter-sunset green,
The hidden pools she passed by when she fled,
The mud flats iridescent as the sheen
Of watered silk over the broad cove spread—
All these will bring her back. Meanwhile we peer
About the house, wide open, left behind
For our delight; the massive ledges sheer,
Rising like pillars, the brown kelps iodined,
Filling our nostrils with the low-tide smells
That waken memory like forgotten bells.

III. HALF TIDE

You are different every morning, rocky shore—
Today the half-tide ledges barely show,
Awash with hurrying wavelets that restore
The lacquer quick as sunlight bids it go.
Now periwinkles on yellow rockweed clinging
Like slates of schoolboys turn from black to gray:
Now rockweed blobs explode as we come bringing
The dark blue clams before the rising bay.
You are a promise of more rocks laid bare,
A promise of more ledges to erase,
A middle ground between the here and there,
A child of Neptune with a Janus face.
One loves the ocean brimming, one low tide;
Here for an hour both are satisfied.

Sport

Five loons maneuvered near my camp—so near
The shore that I could mark the graceful curve
Of each proud neck, the dots around each ear,

Their diving as they formed in line to swerve
Through geometric puzzles of surprise,
Teasing the tiny fledgling of the flock,
Their laugh, as fright was gathering in his eyes,
Assuring him all was well. Over the rock
A cottager whose rifle glittered bright
Patrolled for days in careless mood the shore,
Sniping away at everything in sight—
My dark quintet comes round the camp no more;
But one is left—the fledgling—and his cries
Would bring his mother back, could dead loons rise.

Driftwood

Wave-weary driftwood—stemming from who knows where?
Perhaps a stanchion left at the headland's verge,
Caught by a tide that swept the shore line bare
On a wintry midnight when the full moon's urge
Drove it out of bounds; perhaps a vessel's plank
Caught on a jagged reef, battered and torn,
While the stricken crew launched little boats and sank
Amid the tumult. Howsoever borne,
Today as smooth as popple stones, and bleached
As white as any bone, you cap the coast,
Reposing as if somehow you had reached
Ultima Thule—content to be the host
To idle summer folk whose evening aim
Is song about your bright vermilion flame.

In a Paris Church

The resonant click of shoes on worn stone floors,
Worn deeper at the Stations of the Cross;
Mild crepe-veiled women gliding through the doors,
Perturbed or sad, as if no friendly moss
Had eased their paths in youth; each drops a mite

And flames one candle more; while unaware
Of all around, a bent priest, stoled in white,
Treads back and forth, absorbed in evening prayer.

And one, whose mind the new-world winds of March
Have sung through and swept clean as canyon walls
From creed and dogma, sits beneath an arch
Apart, and wonders what strange essence falls
From this lit altar, purging every aisle,
Giving these old-world hearts the strength to smile.

At Mont-Saint-Michel

Down from Mont-Saint-Michel when sunset traced
The Abbey window panes with green and gold,
Two sable-suited monks devoutly paced
Far out upon the desert sand to hold
Converse of things eternal: one, a youth,
The Emmäus-journey marvel in his eyes;
The other ancient, steadfast in the Truth
Preached on the Mount for fifteen centuries.

High on the Rock, in vision, reappears,
Through dusk inpouring like a great spring tide,
A line of kings spanning a thousand years,
To view the station of their former pride:
Their pomp is gone; but sons of Saint Aubert
Still walk the selfsame sands and speak his prayer.

Granite

Lie on these rocks—perhaps to your surprise
Will spread the glowing comfort of their arms;
Lean on these rocks that lavishly devise
A resting place where odors from the barms
Of ocean, floating in on either side,
Quicken your vision up and down the bay

Of medricks crying, ledges where the tide
Curves round the harbor in a long white spray.
Gaze on these rocks, and know how they are worn
Smooth by the iteration of the sea,
Like the smooth cheeks of aged toilers born
Along this coast whose buffetings may be
The secret of the granite hardihood
That makes them look on life and call it good.

The Hungry Shark

In sixteen hundred and ninety-four,
A hammerhead shark from the Labrador
Took a voyage south, and grew so lean
He could chew the scuppers off a barkentine.
He saw a pirate heave-to a ship,
Smiled as he watched her colors dip—
And under the place where he had no chin
The shark was a-tucking of his napkin in.

"There is only one thing, one thing to do,"
Said Captain Kidd, "get rid of this crew;
They are eating our grub and drinking our rum,
And praying each night for Kingdom Come.
Bring her to, old mate, you skin and bones,
Let's billet them down with Davy Jones"—
And under the place where he had no chin
The shark was a-tucking of his napkin in.

He bound their hands with wet rawhide,
Pushed out a plank far over the side,
Stood by with cutlass gleaming and said,
"Now walk the plank or you lose your head."
The hungry shark pushed his head from the sea
And cried, "O Pirate, have mercy on me."
And under the place where he had no chin
He fell to a-tucking of his napkin in.

146

Each tar with his hands behind his back
Was prodded on with a whack! whack! whack!
Tumbled in the water with a terrible splash,
And turned in a jiffy to corned-beef hash.
The blood floated up on the Caribbean blue,
Around the ship great buzzards flew—
And under the place where he had no chin
The shark was a-tucking of his napkin in.

He hied him back to the Polar Zone,
Fattened on Vikings' blood and bone—
Their blood is sweet, their meat is nice,
Frozen hard in the Arctic ice.
But he loves to remember the trip he took
To Dry Tortugas and Sandy Hook—
And under the place where he has no chin
He falls to a-tucking of his napkin in.

Connecticut Tercentenary Ode

I

What offering can we bring
To the pioneers who made this valley ring
With psalm and sword three centuries ago?
The broadaxe in the river towns proclaimed
Saint George adventuring forth once more to slay
The dragons that were challenging his way
To Liberty and Justice, setting free
Man's urge in separate molds to shape his plea
That Heaven's will be tabernacled here.
Connecticut was Jordan and the clear
Streams flowing to it marked the Promised Land.
Here Hooker, Stone, and Ludlow took their stand
And reared a Western tower that withstood
The dragons of rebellion, fire, and flood.

II

A heritage to honor! As the oak
That hid the Charter from an acorn grew,
So from the Fundamental Orders broke
The twig our fathers planted to renew
The faith of men in nations. Yggdrasill
Of Western soil, shed leaves of healing still!

III

The hills conspired to drive the grimness out
Of hearts too soon aware of savage death;
Men roaming through the pastures, ringed about
With blooms of laurel, breathing its sweet breath,
Were never more content with door or panel
Where beauty was denied its bead or channel.
These homes our fathers cherished, like their laws,
Reveal the steady minds of men who caught
Life's dignity and beauty: freezing, thaws,
Time's negligence, and scars blind worms have wrought
Have sagged their oak foundations, yet they stand
The architectural glory of the land.

IV

Gloom settled on the pioneers to see
The all too transient Oriental glow
Of full-flung autumn on each wayside tree
After a night of rain, fade out and go.
(How could such foliage fling
Defiance to the sky and fail to bring
Down on its head cold winter's reckoning?)
They watched the trees turn gray through countless falls
And poured their heart's blood into gray stone walls.
These walls their Pyramids; the Sphinx that gazed
Upon them from the green, the white church spire,
Whose priests curtailed the Liberty they praised,
And dangled over Everlasting Fire
The Pequots and the witches who defied
The Hebrew God their stern faith magnified.

148

V

Whence came the sternness? Was it from the rocks
That pauperized their hillsides? Or the soil
So thin it set young men to making clocks
Or peddling Yankee notions? Did it coil
Out of the whirlwind gusts of cold that stormed
Hard pews in meetinghouses never warmed?
Grim were the hardships, treacherous the foes
Our fathers grappled with to make them strong;
Out of their poverty and faith arose
A breed that to the Iron Days belong.
Gaze on their portraits, trace deep lines that spent
Long nights in Doubting Castle with Despair;
Heed earnest eyes to whom the heavens had sent
A sign like Jacob's when he strove in prayer.

VI

How numerous the heroes crowd this vale!
A Revolutionary Muse might sing
The blue-eyed teacher-athlete, Nathan Hale;
Or "Brother Jonathan" whose echoes ring
As true as Washington's who called him friend
When friends were few and trusted leaders fled;
Or Putnam, ambushed, wheeling to descend
Precipitous steps; or Silas Deane who sped
DeKalb and Lafayette when many a head
Was bowed to meet an ignominious end.

VII

Another with a fancy more perverse
Might sing the exploits of the untamed few
With habits not so steady: Arnold's curse
To him hides not the blessing. He would do
Obeisance to the name of old John Brown,
To Alcott smiting pedagogues of woe;
To P. T. Barnum tearing the black gown
From Puritanic shoulders—there to throw

A bright burnoose of merriment and cheers
On folk who reckoned earth a pilgrimage of tears.

VIII

Our fancies, rather, let us weave around
The men who hewed the rafters and the beams,
Who served with Mason on Long Island Sound,
And drove the imperturbable ox teams;
Round sailors bearing lilacs from the far
And fragrant Orient
To merge at last their sweet, exotic scent
And color with New England eyes and hair.
How many a cellar yawns whose lilac tree
Can conjure up the scene for you and me!
Tumbled the walls and hearthstone; tough scrub oak
And hardy maple do their best to blind
Our hearts to these our people left behind:
Here is the record no success can bring
To glorious fruition. Lilac, cling
To your abandoned yard and broken wall
Lest we forget the wormwood and the gall
Steeped from New England hemlock. Reinvoke
The memory of the days before the yoke
Fell on unequal shoulders. Give to the breeze
Your heart-shaped blossoms, may they tell what tears
And laughter rounded out three hundred years
Of new-world story from whose page we scan
The enduring grief and dignity of man.

Valediction

Let there be sea gulls crying when I go,
Let there be great waves crumbling on the shore,
Crumbling in sheets like walls of Jericho,
The orchestration of whose ram's-horn score
Kindled my boyhood fancy. Let there be
Gray clouds low hanging over ocean foam—
Soft curtains veiling white sails out at sea,

150

Under the sails far mariners hurrying home
On tides that flood for them and ebb for me.
And let there be fulfillment of the dream
Of Lost Atlantis, once so Easter-bright
I all but reached it on the warm Gulf Stream
That flowed through me. Come, Stream, and warm my flight
When I go out to meet the enfolding night.

MAINE TIDES

Preface

The New England village of a generation ago is almost inconceivable to the youngsters of today. The village was a detached unit, compelled to depend largely upon itself for social existence. English habits must have been strong upon us, for the pattern of the English country gentleman unconsciously dominated our activities. Hunting, fishing, and sailboating occupied a great deal of our time. To the grownups these were largely utilitarian sports, but to boys in their teens they were unadulterated pleasures. The barn chamber was full of dried cod all winter, which meant that "fish and potatoes" figured disproportionately in our diet. The first approach to poetry this author ever heard was:

> "Fish and potatoes, the fat of the land,
> If you can't eat that, you can starve and be damned."

And the mattresses and pillows we slept on were stuffed with the feathers of sea birds ourselves had shot. Consequently the humanitarian aspect of bird slaughter meant little or nothing to us. A coot stew for supper and a feather bed to sleep on afterward were realities that crowded the humanitarian values out. If it was a narrow and circumscribed existence, we, growing up, were little aware of our confinement.

The shadow of John Calvin was always hovering over us. The village atheist, usually the most philosophical member of the community, was one of our crew, and we knew, of course, that he was headed straight for Hell. The grocery-store loafers were less vociferous than the village atheist, but they hunted rabbits on Sunday afternoons and were severely critical always of the devout churchgoers. The only laughter most of us ever heard in the village chapel was on the occasion of a church supper, and the only spiritual excitement we knew came at the time of the periodical "revival"— an event that crowded the pews each night and concluded with a large number of "converts," most of whom turned into "backsliders" as soon as the "evangelist" had left. During these upheavals we read the Bible constantly, if only for purposes of argument, and became well acquainted with the Scriptures.

The women figured largely in the protracted meetings, although they figured hardly at all in other village activities. Looking back at the annual events of the village, many of us pity most of all the fate of the women. Ours was a man's world. The girls never went in swimming with us, as girls do nowadays, possibly because we always went in naked; and scarcely a woman of our acquaintance ever went hunting or sailboating. They did play a large role at the Thanksgiving dinners and the Christmas festivals, but all other activities except, perhaps, the dance, were kept at a strictly masculine level. Many of the finest girls in town would not go to the Saturday night dances at all (the church frowned on their participation) and those girls who did were often suspect. Nevertheless the dances were a great source of enjoyment, and two-thirds of the numbers at these affairs were of the "square" variety which later became almost extinct. We danced the Boston Fancy, the Portland Fancy, Hull's Victory, Lady of the Lake, Fisher's Hornpipe, and other such measures. The more ambitious young people learned the waltz, the two-step, and the schottische, but the bashful and the awkward youngsters essayed only the "squares." The music was largely local (like everything else), but once a year we hired an orchestra from the city eight miles away and had a grand ball, an event that was a landmark in our lives. Entertainment in the village was incredibly meagre, as the author has written elsewhere: a minstrel troupe, a traveling bear, an Indian Remedy Company—these could be counted on to show up in the town hall once a year. As for the rest, the neighbors had to provide it themselves.

Poets who have written about the village have tended to glorify it too much or else dwell too heavily on its shame. In English poetry Goldsmith's *Deserted Village* romanticized Sweet Auburn until it resembled nothing that ever was on sea or land. George Crabbe in his ambition to "paint the cot/As truth would paint it and as bards would not" went to the other extreme. His village was a veritable almanac of calamities. In American poetry one discerns the same tendency. James Whitcomb Riley painted the American village to suit the taste of American businessmen off making money in the great city, at the moment, perhaps, when they looked out of a tenth-story window and wondered whether the dogwood back home were yet in bloom. And Edgar Lee Masters, as an antidote to Riley and his pink-and-white crew, gave us the scandals, the hypocrisies, the abortions that Riley never mentioned. If anything, the extremes of these American writers are even more violent than the extremes of Goldsmith and Crabbe. This is especially unfortunate because the village people themselves, by their very existence, are in no way geared and gaited for extremes. Their lives are not violent, and their way is just what Thomas Gray said it was, one of "even tenor." Floods, northeast storms, blizzards are things they know, but villagers always think of them as exceptional acts of God that are somehow uncalled for in the scheme of things.

In this book the author has tried to avoid extremes. The habitual mood of New England landscape is that of a mild pastel shade, exquisitely delicate but not in any way violent. The tints on the sea are richer, especially at sunrise and sunset; consequently one will be more aware of the sea than he will of the land in perusing this volume, for it was the sea that instilled in the author the desire for expression in poetry. If the reader feels that the activities recorded in Part I are too much idealized, he should remember that most of these *genre* pictures are told from the reminiscent point of view of a boy in his teens. The boy was young and the world was young; the village was integrated, and what went on in the great world outside was of little or no concern to him. From the point of view of a world hamstrung by dictators, life in a little New England seaport a generation ago was life in a Golden Age.

PART I

Cooting

October's ribbons reddening pasture lanes,
And rabbit hounds *ow-owing* on the hills
Stirred hunting passions in us once again.
Each night we hung about the store to hear
The lobster-catchers' "Coots around The Stallion!"
And when the longed-for word at last was spoken,
Straight from the barn waddled our dusty tollers,*
Wanting a coat of paint, some wanting heads,
And all in need of titivating new.
Night after night drawn up to the kitchen table
We tinkered with their ills, and crimped our shells,
With expectation brighter in our minds
Than the loading tools that glinted more each hour.

*A coast word for decoys.

Here the untrammelled moment—fancies woke
And tumbled into boasting: how the coots
Would fall beneath our aim; how sheldrakes, teal,
Sea duck and old-squaws, brant, and even wild goose
Would decorate the yard when we got home.
To match this boasting we would crowd our shells
With more than necessary shot and powder—
"Loading for bear," we young ones kept repeating
Till driven to bed, and there we tossed and turned
For fear the men would row away without us.

Fragrance of coffee lured us to the kitchen
Where, told to speak in whispers, we evoked
An unaccustomed atmosphere—a tone
Of deep suppressed excitement that submerged
The very walls and curtains of the room.
Out in the yard we felt the deathly chill
Of four o'clock and drew our bodies in,
Contracting to the coming on of winter.
Down to the shore we clambered; rubber boots
Banging the frozen ground set roosters crowing
Defiance to the desolating chill
Of air that stung and numbed. Still dark was the bay
When we picked up the gunning rock and moored
Among brown kelps our painted wooden tollers.
Dragging the dory in well out of sight,
Each took his hiding place when quick from the ocean
Darted a flock of coots straight for our snare,
Taxiing forward in a wake of spray.
Aware of our deceit, they stretched to fly,
And as they rose we banged a sudden salvo
That waked the slumbering bay for miles around.
The chill of morning vanished as we spied
Four patchheads drifting toes up on the foam.
The rose-red sun bisecting the horizon
Smiled in upon our ledge and on our faces,
And we were happy as young savages
Back in the early sunrise of the world.

The birds kept coming on, and all our guns
Grew hot with action. No more talk of cold,

Or shoving fingers underneath the armpits
Before removing shells. The rising tide
And rising sun together welled around
That ledge as if its lonely isolation
Demanded lustier currents of flood tide
And livelier lavishment of morning sun
Than all the others sleeping in the channel.
Burnt-orange draperies on the morning sky
Turned, as the sun rose, to a salmon pink;
And when a flock of black coots with white wings
Against that saffron curtain wheeled and lit
Beside our tollers in the blue and gold
Of first flood tide, I laid aside my gun
And eastward gazed, indifferent to chiding
I knew would come, soon as the shooting ended.
A bigger game was calling, with a cry
More piercing than the cry of coots and old-squaws
Circling above us—quarry more elusive
Than hunters for blue goose or wild sea eagles
Or even ibises could ever know.

Cod-Fishing

" 'Tis time we got rigged up for laying in
Our winter fish," an uncle would begin;
"The flies are gone and we can now salt slack."
He gave us little peace till we were back
Into the bay a second time. New snoods
Were bent on new hooks; from the neighboring woods
We cut spruce limbs and shaped them into reels,
Filed sharp our old hooks, punched new leads; for creels
We brought out tubs and tierces—autumn fun
Meant food for winter and gay sport in one
Exciting day's adventure. (Pity him
Who makes his winter fishing just the grim
And driving need of sustenance—his day
Is never famished who turns work to play.)

We knew the favorite shoals where kelps appeared
At dead low water and profusely reared
Protective aprons whose soft shades of brick
And brown were cunningly designed to trick
The cod's worst enemies. We chose a day
When low-tide slack at sunrise found the bay
Free from disturbing groundswell; chose for bait
A large white clam, the main course; then a crate
Of small black lobsters just about to shed,
More tempting than the clams; we knew a bed
Of big blue mussels on a half-tide reef
And raided it as we rowed out. The chief
Of all our secret morsels never came
Into the light, nor could you guess its name.

The older men shuck clams as we row out,
And sunrise finds us there. A lusty shout
Comes from the boy who lands his first rock cod;
He boasts his prowess, even says "By God"
In his excitement. The proud father's frown
And firm rebuke can scarcely bring him down
To solid earth; but soon his uncle's line
Sags with a twenty-pounder, and the shine
On the boy's face dims to see the two fish rub,
Flopping together in the bottom of the tub.
Then two haul stroke by stroke, and he who lands
The bigger of the two calls on all hands
To witness his superior fishing power.
Thus passes all too soon the slack-tide hour
Before the fish ease off their ravenous zeal
And our own hunger wakens. We boys steal
A bite with one hand, fishing with the other,
Till apple pie comes out, at which we smother
Our passion for handlining, and attend
An earlier passion's keen-as-fishhook end.

Two sharpen knives and gut the fish, and two
Bend to the oars, when over streaks of blue
The air about us is alive with white
And pale blue sea gulls, as if morning light
Under the mackerel sky had found a dress

In which to body all its loveliness.
They give us wings; our arms no longer tire
Pulling the oars—we feel the living fire
Of beauty as they swoop and dip and flock
Around us; and no power on earth can lock
The door then opened in the mind of one
Who saw what wings were holding up the sun.

Thanksgiving Shoot

Thanksgiving time we made a festival
That never should have lapsed. Two natural leaders
Divided all men fit for bearing arms,
And some unfit, in two contending camps
Of friendly rivalry. Their names were posted,
And hunters of the past, whose guns were hanging
Cobwebby round their muzzles, were assigned
The honored task of judging. On the paper
A list was drawn depicting in round numbers
The count of every bird or animal
Brought in before the stroke of six—the prize,
A turkey dinner free to all who won
Paid by the team that lost. The smaller birds—
Devil-divers, water-witches, dippers,
Sea-myrrh and whistlers, pegging-awls and plover,
Along with rabbit, partridge, mink and muskrat,
Were listed fifty; coots, sea ducks and drakes,
Black ducks and sheldrakes, loons and laughing gulls,
Tallied a hundred each; brant goose two hundred;
Wild goose and fox, shyer than other game,
Were listed at a thousand points apiece,
And he who bagged one that day owned the village.
We boys were more on tiptoe than the men—
Up bright and early, questioning the hunters
With questions altogether out of order,
Yelling our heartiest wishes to them all,
Some to the woods, some to the waters speeding.
They shared our fresh abandon, though the code

Made audible expression of their mood
A joy denied. A few with reputations
To be maintained escaped our wild salute
By hurrying off between pitch-dark and dawn.
And some whose marksmanship made them the butt
Of hunting gossip, lingered in the village
And shuttlecocked our saucy battledore
With dialogue that soon enough was passed
From mouth to mouth—thus fastening cap and bells
On our autumnal crown of rivalry.

Meanwhile the women of the village planned
A harvest banquet. Pies, and cakes, and puddings—
Rich Indian puddings, and lush pumpkin pies—
Involving keener rivalry, were carried
Into the village hall and spread around
On wooden tables mounting wooden horses
Stretching from stage to door. (The women felt
The need of festive hours.) At half-past five
Excitement rolled in waves along the hall.
The hunters storming in with coots and rabbits
Slung on the barrels of their guns; the judges
Solemn as a row of Indian braves,
Examining the game with silent care
To make sure every animal or bird
Was freshly killed; the spirited dispute
About some bird or animal not listed,
Climaxed by the appeal to Silas Hall
Whose reputation for integrity
A circuit judge might envy; the surprise
When our loved country doctor ambled in
Just as the chapel clock was striking six,
With game enough to foil the settled winners;
No monarch ever swaggered to his throne
With quite the air of Doctor Horne the day
He turned the tide and crowned his hunting mates
Victorious—old beams and rafters shook
Before his stride. Fragrance of basted turkey
Rising like steam above the four long tables;
The blessing spoken in a livelier tone
Than we had bargained for; the ironic banter

162

From team to team before the men fell to;
The questioning of Doctor Horne's credentials;
And over all the flood tide of good will
Rising on dun-gray flats of late November,
Marked this our foremost autumn festival,
When Nature, lowering brilliant flags and pennants,
Signaled the need of gayer colors within.

Smelting

The milder souls to whom the autumn sea
Was always rimmed about with treachery
Sought recreation in a long green cove
Where tidewaters with emptying brooklets strove,
Pursuing golden smelts—a dainty dish
For every connoisseur of toothsome fish.
There when the autumn rains were at their height,
And muddy waters curtained from our sight
Whatever swam beneath, we each one took
A pole and dip net, and an extra hook
And grape basket whose cover showed a hole
Cut by a jackknife where the flipping toll
Could be slipped lengthwise through. Our first delay
Was at the cove's head where the minnows play
In brackish pools. Though tutored in their pranks
Of darting underneath the clayey banks,
We plunged our dip nets here and there below
The edges of the pool, uncertain how
Our luck would fare. Often a vigorous dip
Revealed that they had given us the slip—
Then we would scour the bank from edge to edge.
Again the net came dripping from the sedge
With four or five soft bellies flipping white
Against the black mesh, and a quick delight
Swam in our eyes. A few rods on we found
An earlier group stood on the very ground
Ourselves had chosen to fish from, and far worse,
We sometimes heard a dreaded Irish curse
Heaped on our heads for "blethering loud noise

And scaring off the fishes." Youthful poise
That makes a quick recovery soon found us,
And we took second-best places. All around us
Were poles extending outward from the bank
And bobbers drifting up and down. The plank
Of quietness that reached to every hook
Bridged all the gaps of this particular nook,
The striking of a match the biggest sound
Heard for an hour on that boggy ground.
Quiet the cove lay, mottled green and brown,
Only a maple leaf slow drifting down
Brightened the muddy waters. On the face
Of the cove was scarcely ripple enough to trace
Which way the wind was stirring. On each line
Of stout black thread the sinkers met the brine
In perfect stillness; and the smelts' own gold—
Scorning the brilliant color of the scrolled
Illumination of the mint—aligned
Its tone and shade to those of nuggets mined
In quiet Northern creeks. One dream of peace
That haunts me as a permanent release
From noisy traffic, floats about the balm
Of autumn smelting—with a flood-tide calm
And tranquil rain descending drowsily
On that long inlet hidden from the sea.

Wood-Chopping

The deepening cold impelled us to the wood lot
With axes, saws, and wedges. Choosing clumps
Of spruce, birch, hemlock, larch, and stout rock maple,
(Maple whose flame-red foliage in October
Made plausible the burning bush of Moses),
We found a warmth on cold December days
No airtight parlor stove could duplicate—
A warmth of sunlight over sheltering boughs,
Made hourly warmer by the swinging axe
Scattering spices of Arabia
Over New England shores. The busy hum

164

Of busy men was music we could follow:
The *pianissimo,* the trimming up
Of brittle limbs, or muted snap of brushwood
Burning in little piles; the higher *wheen*
Of crosscut saws in heavy birch logs singing;
Fortissimo when well-ground helves drove deep
Through knotted trunks; the *grand finale* when
A haughty monster cracking at its base
Swept forward with increasing rush and roar
Snapping off limbs of smaller trees, down-crashing;
And in its wake the bravos of the men
That one more whore of Babylon was mastered—
These filled the landscape with such moving sound
We quite forgot the sharp December chill,
Forgot the frozen ground encased in snow
Whose drifts of varying depths made walking treacherous,
Though not too treacherous for the boys who sank
Crotch-deep in white to gain this sanctuary.
How few could keep away! The rich aroma
Of pipe tobacco, burning underbrush,
And fresh-hewn chips of spruces, blended, gave
The spot an atmosphere as dear to us
As Gothic-spired cities yield to boys
Born in cathedral shadows. With what surprise
Some little patch of ground new-cleared would stir
The live roots of our hearts! Was it the way
The earth curved round a central knoll, or grouped
Its contours underneath a few white birches
That stood as if in meditative awe
At such a happy sight? Or was it rather
Texture of moss and turf unrolled beneath
Clearings of bright blue sky, revealing there
How exquisite cup-candle moss could be,
After weeks of blossoming in the shade,
When morning sun set off its red-trimmed tapers
With undiluted light?
                The larger growth
We ranged in cordwood piles—each cord exact—
The handle of the axe our measuring rod,
"From peak to scarf," our phrase of honest measure.
The sapling growth above gray moss and ledges

We threw in mammoth piles—the best to go
For weir stakes in the spring; the gnarled and twisted
To fuel kitchen fires. Melting snow
Gave warning for the sleds to snake it out,
A task assigned by honored understanding
To semi-superannuated neighbors
No longer keen for strenuous pursuits.

One afternoon when all the rest had gone
I lingered in the woods to watch the sunset,
And through the leafless birches just at dusk
Saw mounds of snow flaunt pink and violet shadows,
While one wide band of green along the west
Flung out the emerald fringe white birches called for.
There as I stood, girdled in afterglow,
Still as the stately birch that stood beside me,
Out of a thicket hopped a hare. Unhurried
He stopped and gazed as if he felt the glory,
Then went his way. Scarcely a moment later
A partridge flew into an upper bough
Of this one tree and budded. These companions,
By some strange alchemy of winter magic,
Transformed wood-chopping to a sacred rite
Performed on ceremonial greenwood altars,
Whose liturgy invested me with vigor
Against the disillusion of the years.

Village Christmas

The blue and pink of sunrise through black boughs
Of scraggly apple trees behind the house
Was in itself enough to draw us thence—
But over the crusted snow's half-hidden fence
The gold of spruces, fresh as in mid-May,
Luring us toward our happiest holiday,
Transferred that pink tint out of crusted snow
Into our youthful faces with a glow
No poverty could dim. Three dark days more
And Christmas Eve would sparkle up the shore

Like golden sun shafts on a leaden sea
That break through black clouds unexpectedly
And from a funnel pour a glittering heap
Of precious coins making the billows leap
And jostle one another for their share.
We chose a tree symmetrically fair
That tapered toward the summit like a cone;
Admiring, praised the knack ourselves alone
Possessed in picking spruces; felled another
Not quite so fair, but fit to be a brother
To this first lady of our Christmas choice,
And, unaware, made everyone rejoice
As we noised up the street in swaggering haste,
Up to the little chapel where we placed
Them either side the pulpit. There they stood
Even more beautiful than in the wood;
Their green boughs touched with sunlight and their smell,
More spicy here than down beyond the well,
Scattering myrrh and incense round our door.
Their boughs, bedecked by aging hands, soon bore
Festoons of silvery tinsel, socks of gauze
With fruit and candy crammed. Who would not pause
Before such loveliness? Who could not guess
Why man once worshipped in the wilderness
These messengers that cheered his hearth with fires
And wreathed a thousand hills with stately spires
To lift his weary spirit to the skies?

The trees in full regalia, and the day
Creeping toward three o'clock, we found our way
Obstructed by the janitor with a broom.
He "had his orders" to patrol the room
And let no child down front. We all stood clear,
Like gamins when a steamboat hits the pier,
Wondering what our biggest gift would be.
Alas for ever-present poverty!
That gift the one and only for a few
Whose treasure ships were always overdue;
And for a smaller few no craft would dock—
Only the cornball-fruit-and-candy sock
The Sunday School Committee had prepared

Would reach these spawn of Satan, scraggly-haired,
Who sprawled along the outskirts of the hills
In shacks with rag-stuffed windows, sagging sills.

Throughout the gathering dark of that short day
The old folks went up front with bundles gay,
Self-consciously important, paused and spoke
In tones of secrecy as if the yoke
On Santa's shoulders were too much to bear,
And they were anxious to assume a share.
Under the boughs throughout the afternoon
Their toilworn faces shone as if a moon
Too long away from earth had risen once more
And shed its radiance over sea and shore.
Three families vied to see which one could make
The gaudiest exhibit. But why take
Time to tell of these? The fifty others
In poverty's wide bond were neighbors, brothers,
And brothers of the Master whose command
The lowly were the first to understand;
They loved the spirit that perpetuated
This festival through wintry days deep-freighted
With frozen sand that clogged the glass of time.

By seven our grim band was clogged with rhyme,
For "speaking pieces" was a ritual
To be put on whatever else befell
Our Christmas Eve. We marched up on the stage
(Combating inwardly a secret rage)—
Like little puppets bowed and looked around
Over a reach of faces, blushed and ground
Our teeth together, gulped a *cul-de-sac*
In our dry throats that would not straighten back
When we began to speak. We gulped again
To the great amusement of our fellowmen
(Except, of course, our parents who had figured
Their offspring brighter than the vast beleaguered
Host of conscripts gone or yet to come!)
Upon that stage of battle there were some
Who spoke with ease, and others so dramatic
They made the rats uneasy in the attic

Of the belfry tower; and one girl made us blush
With her assurance till there came a hush
Over the room, and in the hush a giggle
Quite unexpected from a lass whose wriggle
Revealed a nervous strain of uncontrol;
The dangerous years were gnawing at her soul,
And at her body too. The minister
Looked sternly down the aisle and glared at her
Till she got up and bolted through the door.
The minister arose, sweet oil to pour,
And tried to smile Luella's deed away.
The effort failing, he began to pray.
Above his station in between the trees
A mammoth popcorn ball, a masterpiece,
Upon a line from tree to tree was hung,
The generous thought of Aunt Mahala Young
Who loved the Christmas festival so much
That everything enlarged beneath her touch.
It was as big as children's appetites
Who dream of popcorn balls through winter nights,
And all eyes were upon it. Should I tell?
The janitor had done his work too well,
Had saved out yellow birches for this hour,
And both stoves in the rear drove such a shower
Of heat waves up the aisle the cold molasses
Melted and ran through that great ball's crevasses
Till crash! the cornball struck the preacher's head
And showered its kernels on small children spread
Along the front settees. The older folks
Who reckoned this no interim for jokes,
Restrained themselves superbly, but the boys
Let out such raucous hurricanes of noise
All hands joined in. And then and there some owned
Luella's ruined Christmas stood atoned.

The breathless interlude of hope and fear
When presents are called off, at length is here.
Out from behind the pulpit Santa pops
In bright red suit, black boots with white-rimmed tops
And mask with silvery beard, sings out, "Well, well,"
Entreating silence with his small brass bell.

He first snips off a little pink bisque doll
And reads the name—the favorite girl of all
The toddlers of the village—her blue eyes
And golden hair and deep unfeigned surprise,
Coupled with joy to find the doll her own,
Draw every eye upon her and enthrone
The age-old symbol of the Christmastide
In those who watch her clasp it to her side.
For present number two the Saint pulls out
A small red drum, and with expectant shout
Calls off the name of one who counters, "I
Don't want a drum; I want a knife!" The wry
Expression on his face so fills his mother
With mortifying shame she tries to smother
Her anger in a shawl as each one lifts
His eyes in her direction. Santa shifts
His pacifying tactics, quickly turns
To present number three, though his face burns
Behind the linen mask and in his heart
He pours forth curses on the bold upstart
Who wrecked by one uncastigated trick
His chance to be acclaimed as one Saint Nick
The village would remember. Half in rage
He dives among the presents on the stage
And brings out offerings of the well-to-do,
Reading them in such haste that he is through
With all three families before the rest
Have time to be sufficiently impressed.
The sought effect is further ruined when
A pig's tail wrapped with care for Uncle Ben
Rolls laughter through the crowd, and marks amen
To one more Christmas Eve. A few look sad,
Their longings bent on things they might have had;
But one boy is so happy with new skates
He tries them on, compares them with his mate's
New shiny pair, concludes his own are best,
And has them on his boots when he is pressed
To rise and hurry home.
                              Out on the snow
The winter moon is pouring a white glow;
The stars are brilliant as they were the night

170

The Prince of Peace was born; the fields as bright.
The horses stirring round the chapel door
Are anxious for the stable; small bells pour
Their tinkle on the frost, and children's voices
Persuade one that the earth itself rejoices
In such a swelling outburst of good will
As floods this night with heavenly music still.

Fox Hunt

How many a web can Time alone unweave!
Unraveled now, the tangle of a morning
That fubbed the clumsy fingers of a boy.

After an all-night level fall of snow
That cheered the face of the sun to look upon,
Two youngsters, breathless, set us all agog
Announcing fox tracks on Mosquito Island,
And we shoved off with shotguns, hounds, and Cyrus—
The master huntsman never left behind.

Our beagles, overjoyed to be unleashed,
Bellowed their gladness on the tingling air,
As we took stations on a narrow cut-down
That cleft the wooded island. What a chance
For one of us when Mister Fox crossed over!
Soon yelping echoes traveled through gray cliffs,
And over silver-coated stumps and logs,
And louder, nearer, nearer, louder sounded.
Then all at once a stillness swept the clearing,
And brushed the tenseness from our eager faces,
A stillness mellower than quilts of snow
Bending young spruces to a crouching quiet.

"Call in the dogs. We may as well go home!"
Shouted our senior partner with a smile—
The smile, a puzzle to our cheated minds,
The words, from him, as good as a command,
So down to the clean-swept ledges of the beach
We plodded, disappointed, through deep snow.

Nearest the shore, already I had seen
A floating patch of seaweed driving fast
Against the current; ebb tide running strong,
And this dark object furrowing straight against it
Ruffled me as a rip tide ruffles a bight.
I hailed our elder brother, "Over here!
Come, see this freak of Nature." Down he came,
Took one sharp look, then chuckled till his body
Shook with joy as deep as my disgust.

"You goose, you passed up one chance of a lifetime.
That fox was grinning in the very muzzle
Of your new gun, then wrapping up his nose
In that convenient patch of floating seaweed,
Guessed he would ferry over to the main.
See his two ears pushed out above the tide!
He's given us the slip, and here we are,
Stranded on this island high as Haman."

Puzzled as I was then, today I know
And understand the laughter in the eyes
And voice of that old huntsman we revered.
Against the ebbing tide that thinned his blood
His will was struggling like the struggling fox,
Both hard beset by the same dread enemy
Whose pace is all too sure. Though one with us
Out of old habit and the pride we took
In his clean marksmanship, that day his heart
Was treading with the fox against the tide,
The awful tide of dark and bitter water—
Stirred to the depths by this brave spectacle,
This dauntless bundle of life outwitting Death.

Interlude

On days when grass was crystallized with snow
In deep midwinter we would often go
To see the untroubled woods. What friendlier sight

172

Could burst on us? Snow waiting to alight
On snow already caked in frozen clumps
Like cotton-batting rolls, the many stumps
Of spruces sawed off knee-high years before;
Above our shoulders evergreen branches bore
Streaks of white with purple shadows blent;
And at our feet shell ice, all water spent
Among brown roots, a crystal whiteness lent
To weave a rich mosaic in the shade.
The light and darkness all about us made
The grove an Indian rug with orange braid
Where Pocahontas' ghost might sit and brew
A medicine for John Smith's phantom crew.

Then walking toward the village, halfway out
A swan's-down shower circled us about
With feathery flakes that spiraled down, to stop
And circle back like white spume on the top
Of powerful waves when all the wind is gone
And only undertow keeps churning on—
The world was everything that we could want,
Stilled in a hush four walls could never grant;
Within us there was lit a quiet glow,
Lit by the pure white sparks of falling snow—
Inviolate hour, quick to blend and run,
Under the mildness of a curtained sun,
The elements of earth and sky in one.

Winter Evenings

Darkness came on at four. We set a lamp
In the middle of the drop-leaf kitchen table
And ate our homemade bread with raspberry jam,
Or black molasses from a jug whose cold
Unwillingness to drain dragged out the meal,
While fine-split kindling in the airtight stove
Two rooms away scattered a glowing cheer.
The hanging lamp, with ruby-spangled glass,
Was shining there, and there we went to play

At pinochle, old maid, parchesi, authors,
And checkers, monarch of our indoor games.
The older men, contemptuous of these pastimes,
Clung to their chairs around the kitchen table
"In thoughts more elevate, and reasoned high
Of Providence, Foreknowledge, Will, and Fate—
Fixed fate, free will, foreknowledge absolute—
And found no end, in wandering mazes lost."

Our mother's voice that knew the place of tears
Stirred dreams in us through many a winter evening
While snow moaned round the eaves as if to find
Wind-hovering ghosts of loved ones lost at sea.
She read while we all sat around and listened—
Some knitting pot-heads for the coming spring;
Some dipping into a tierce of tamarinds
Brought by a captain from a lazier shore.
With her a favorite was the wayward Celt
Who wove his fancy's fiber into the warp
And woof of Wakefield's unsuspecting vicar,
Who sang in flowing couplets of the Traveler—
A brother to our own brass-buttoned few—
Our few whose binnacles across the world
Showed compasses with bright magnetic needles
Pointing unvaryingly toward ports of home.

No other tale we listened to in childhood
Stirred us so much as that of Uncle Tom
And little Eva in the book that swayed
The nation's judgment forty years before.
We wept as Mother read the cruelties
Of old Legree whose long black lash beat down
Its live tattoo on faithful Uncle Tom;
We crossed with Liza on the uncertain ice;
And saw bright angels round the hanging lamp
When little Eva spoke her ninth farewell.

On moonlit nights a ready troop of friends
Came crowding round our wheezy parlor organ
To sing the melodies of Stephen Foster
And sailor chanties such as "Blow Man, Blow."

The old men in the kitchen held us down
To melancholy hymns on Sunday evenings—
A rule that egged the more adventurous on
To outbursts such as "Turkey in the Straw,"
And more than once we saw old faces smile
At these unsanctioned interludes of song.

The singing crew dispersed, we drew up chairs
To talk of fistic bouts and murder trials.
The ten years' reign of John L. Sullivan
We knew word-perfect like the Ten Commandments;
His mills with Ryan, Corbett, and Kilrain,
His barnstorm tours across the continent,
His temperance jolts when he at last grew sober,
His place among the immortals of the ring.

One murder trial seemed to have no ending,
The Lizzie Borden case, New England's purge
For all the dark suppressions of a century;
A war of words about her trial raged
From Mount Katahdin to the Golden Gate;
And when the trenches circled round our home
The grownups sent us scurrying to bed
That they might talk unhampered half the night.
(Parents, be not deceived—no master builder
Makes walls so thick or curtains so opaque
That they shut out the eyes and ears of children.)
We sat on cold front stairs and heard them tell
Of her rich dress of brightly sequined black;
Of how she fainted when her mother's name
And father's name were mentioned; of her wealth
That grew the more, the more her trial lingered;
Of faithful pastors clinging to each arm
As she walked up Fall River's tiny courtroom.
The tension lessened when a village wag
Broke in upon his neighbors' arguments
By striking up a ditty that delighted
Our cold crew shivering on the dark front stairs:

> Lizzie Borden took the axe
> And gave her mother forty whacks;

And when she saw what she had done,
She gave her father forty-one.

We quivered even more upon the stairs
When murder struck a Maine-built barkentine,
The *Herbert Fuller*, lumber-laden, bound
For far Rosario in southern waters.
The name of Bram, Bram, Bram came sounding through
The downstairs rooms, and up the dark front hall,
And in its wake the victims—Captain Nash,
His wife, and mate, in accents tinged with sorrow.
We heard a sceptic hint of Charlie Brown,
The unlucky steersman on that fatal night,
Debating whether one could leave the wheel,
Commit a threefold murder and return
Before the ship came up into the wind.
Nine bearded captains went to testify
On this one issue, four of whom we knew—
The very men who sailed along our coast,
And anchored near our home in foggy weather.
We crawled in bed to dream about the axe,
The bloody axe that murdered Captain Nash,
His wife, and mate—close by our feet it hung
Suspended like a spectral sword in air.

Supreme among those unforgotten nights
Were those that made time gallop like the tide
When garrulous neighbors made our house their inn.
We felt the mantle of a thousand heroes
Had fallen on us. With ours no tales compared:
Miraculous escapes of fishermen
Caught in the swirling breakers; towering yarns
Of hurricanes that swooped like pirates down
The coast and terrified our shipping—raids
That touched our homes and carried off our boys
Before their threescore ten was one-third ended.
We begged our father tell us once again
How he escaped while crowding too much sail
On *Onaway* the hour a blinding squall
Struck, keeling her over; how, when the cockpit filled,
He quickly drew his pocketknife and cut,

Just in the nick of time, the towboat's painter,
Jumped in and trembled on a white-capped ocean
To see his sloopboat shuttle to her tomb.
We made a neighbor tell a hundred times
Of Howard Blackburn's fate—a Gloucester saga—
Blackburn, the fisherman who lost his ship
Out trawling on the Grand Banks in a dory,
And carefully made certain that his hands
Curled freezing to the oars, rowed on and on
Over the shouldering billows through a snowstorm,
Reaching at length a cove in Newfoundland
A hundred miles away, where he camped down
All winter, nourishing his frozen stumps—
To turn up twelve months later on the Cape,
And harvest fame as a salty tavern keeper.

How often we concluded with that night—
The blackest night that ever rocked our world—
When *Pentagoet, Portland,* and a score
Of lesser craft went down! We knew them all,
And reveled in details that were familiar,
As people in loved verse they know by heart.
The knocking out of ashes in old pipes,
And glances at the little ones which said,
"What, you still up?" were signals for repose;
Then silence in the room brought to our ears
The voice of that old nurse of dreams, the sea.

March Snowstorm

With winter's short month at an end,
And spring town meeting just in sight,
We little dreamed the year would send
A mammoth miracle of white—
Enough to make our world stand still
In fleece above the window sill.

The afternoon of the day before
Was overcast, the usual gray,

We had slight warning of the blast,
Day came and went, another day;
Late afternoon, quick darkness fell,
And Night shook out her wizard spell—

Spell of a myriad white doves
That must have gathered in the sky
All winter, filling empty groves,
Till the time was ripe for them to fly
Earthward in flocks, as if to brood
The shore line into solitude.

These halcyon birds preferred our coast
As their domain—they flew and lit
On every stone wall, tree, and post,
Muffling the elements to fit
Their transmigrations and erase
The wrinkles from earth's tired face,

Folding her in a feathery cape
Softer than robes of fairy queens,
Revealing glories in her shape—
Men marveled at familiar scenes
As the old men at the Scaean gate
Viewed Helen when she passed. Relate

Who will the whiteness of that morn,
Our hearts were set on things to do:
Give cows their hay, and hens their corn,
See that the road was broken through
For the mail stage blocked on One Mile Hill,
A challenge to our shoveling skill.

We shoveled in a whirl of noise
And moved great barriers off as pay
For taxes. Who would not rejoice
To see both burdens melt away?
Was ever a task before put through
In such a raucous hullabaloo?

178

The children fought for shovels, lost
To grownups—frantic, made appeal
To mothers whose compliance cost
Such deadlocked conference, pact, and deal
As would have made an international
Agreement sound completely rational.

Men's voices, too, rose loud—they joked
At Nature's wayward trick; one fell
To snowballing with the boys; provoked
When a youngster's ball, directed well,
Exploded in his face, he cried,
"You son of a bitch, I'll tan your hide!"

We cut the drifts into marble blocks,
And carved a marble canyon out;
Filled with the spirit that unlocks
Communal forces, puts to rout
Defeat, and dubs lone enterprise
Guerilla warfare in disguise.

We battered down one ten-foot wall—
For the wind had sprung up after four
Twisting the all-night level fall
To cliffs and gullies like our shore—
Together we had once more tied
Our hamlet to the world outside.

Evening found us at the store
Adorning incidents with charms—
The glory of a well-done chore
Brooding above our weary arms;
And sauntering home we saw stars lift
Approving eyes on every drift.

The Revival

When winter's length had stretched itself so long
That stretching had grown irksome, into town

Rode the Evangelist, whose Sunday dress
Of linen shirt, silk tie, and long black coat
(In contrast to the slouchy clothes we wore)
Made women's eyes grow wider, and assured
A fair beginning to the long campaign
Against the trinity that never failed
To keep his Trinity well occupied—
The world, the flesh, and the devil. Let him come;
Most anything was welcome; drifting snow
Had clogged the roads for weeks, and leveled full
Old cellars with a quicksand floor of white.

Dissenting notes came only from the few
Who nightly hung around the grocery store
Wishing it were an Indian remedy show;
They knew these fakirs, marveled at their tricks,
And swallowed yarns of Indian conjurers,
Paying hard-earned coin with open eyes.
But this strange herald of a brighter West
Than any Indian tribe had galloped over
Bred in them faint uneasiness. They went
For want of something better, crowding in
Rear pews and listening to impassioned pleas
With smiles that hesitated on the brink
Of dubbing him a fakir—breaking out
In titters often at his wild outsurge
Of unrestrained emotion—giving way
At other whiles, when he seemed rather sane,
To confirmation of a platitude
Uttered with unctuous finality.

"An easy living his," their spokesman said,
"Dolled up in Sunday-go-to-meeting duds,
No chores to roust him out, no whistle blowing,
No hours of steady labor; sleeping late
And sitting round with womenfolks. I'd like
To have his job." The few about the stove
Whose pipes were not demanding close attention
Assented to the arraignment, but they went
To sing the hymns; nor would they care to miss
New converts straggling to the mercy seat.

Some, desperate in their longing to throw off
Emotional stagnation, troubled sat,
Squirming like children at a grownup dance.
These were the souls this follower of Peter
Would gather in; for them each afternoon
The faithful few before the altar rail
Bent long in prayer; for them each night he fed
His choicest bait: "O sinners, won't you come
Before it is too late; before the worms
Have done their last and deadly work; the doors
And lintels of your homes look safe—but see!
Death hovers in the sky above your heads;
We hear the flapping of his wings, nor know
The day or hour he will swoop. Prepare
To stand before the judgment bar of God.
And you, young folks, not yet embarked on sin,
I feel constrained especially for you.
I know myself the by-path meadows strewn
To lead young feet astray: the gilded dens
Of vice in city slums were dragging me
Into their toils; I looked upon the wine;
The scarlet woman's lips I tasted; down
In sin and degradation did I sink.
But His free grace has washed away my sins,
And He can blot out yours; O sinners, come!"

The exhortation finished, saints arose
To add their pleas; and when the evening call
Was climaxed with the hush of quiet breathing,
Some pent-up sister in a tremulous voice
Struck up, "Just As I Am Without One Plea,"
And down to the mercy seat in tears manoeuvred
The hesitant and half-decided, drawn
Into the port of faith on tides that swept
Their battered hulks where they could cast an anchor.

The service over, back to his room he went
In boisterous humor, threw his Bible down,
And, rubbing palms together, looked around
In a valise to find the book wherein
He kept a record of the souls he won,

And marked them down, as some bold Indian scout
Might notch his gun to keep the tally straight.
On these occasions he was too wrought up
For restful sleep, and, looking for a haven
To idle in, found easy comradeship
In a young blade whose dad was wealthier
Than all our laboring fathers put together.

Behind a thoroughbred filly they drove off,
Long after we had blown out bedroom lamps,
A buffalo robe to fend them from the cold,
Silver bells ringing on the silver air,
For relaxation in a tavern; here
He felt secure—those eight long miles were more
Than eighty are today—for Space was checked
By Time before the adventurous Einstein came
To formulate the law. There by the bar
Of Indian rosewood, right foot on the rail,
His right hand on a glass of Scotch and soda,
In confidence he filled young listening ears
With his frank, tavern-bred philosophy:

"I know I'm not a Dwight L. Moody, Rex;
My father, nothing but a herring-seiner,
Just dragged along from hand to mouth—you know
The way men live along this coast. One day
A man named Jurnegan, all dressed up swell,
Came to Lubec and told the people there
That gold could be extracted from sea water,
And he was all for getting us a pile.
Boy, you should see the mail that came to him,
Crowded with checks, and bills, and money orders,
And him just walking round in gospel black.
I watched him for a week, then said, 'Look here,
This hard bone labor gets you nowhere, sell
Your traps and seines, and be a fisher of men.'
Right then and there I threw my old life down,
And looked around for institutes that gave
A six-months' course for country theologs.
What is it now," he mellowed on his words,
"Makes John D. Rockefeller rich, I ask,

182

Or General Coxey famous? Luck, I say,
Just downright luck, like winning big at poker.
You birds think education helps. It don't.
The only ones who get help out of schools
Are those who don't take schooling seriously;
The rest go in, stay in, and die unknown,
Like monks shut up in cells behind gray walls.
Life's luck; I grab it as it comes; I see
A pretty girl like Jane"—(Rex bristled here,
For he, like us, thought Jane the village treasure,
A Dian we all worshipped)—"You agree,
A man's a fool to pass up girls like her?
You tell me Jane's all right; they're all all right
Till the right man comes along, and I, old pal,
Am the right man more than anyone I know."

After a night like this, the heavy sleep,
He seemed subdued; some deep Bethesda pool
Of righteousness within his soul upheaved
Its depths till they were troubled, and remorse
At wayward living battled in his mind,
Which he would take out on the congregation
In high Hebraic curses like those spoken
Out of the mount in Deuteronomy.
"You scoffers and revilers at the truth
Revealed within the Word of God, beware;
You sniggerers sitting in the scorner's seat
Blaspheming here this holy house of God,
The curse of God must be pronounced on you.
Myself have seen God's patience stretched too far.
One afternoon in Eggemoggin Reach,
A herring-seiner drifting with the tide
Two hours without a breath of wind, took out
A quarter, tossed it in the air, and said,
'I wish the bald-headed Jesus would send me
A quarter's worth of wind.' We stood aghast
To hear the man blaspheme, and wished ourselves
A long way off. Quick as I take to tell
A squall darkened the bay a copper hue,
His topmast bent, then snapped, and fell on deck,
Striking him dead. . . . Take care! God sent me here

Before your hearts are hardened, and the worm
That dieth not has eaten out your pith."

From far and near the people came each night
To see the wonders of the Lord prevail
Against indifference and complacency.
Some who had scarcely spoken to each other
For thirteen years shook hands and grew fast friends.
The village dances lagged, then failed to bring
Enough to pay the fiddler. Spring arrived,
And off the Evangelist went to other fields
That lay ripe to the harvest. Summer bloomed,
The fiddler's music drifted down the street;
Backsliders multiplied till only three
Of those who saw the light remained to pray
With the somber company who kept the faith.

One late fall evening when the winds blew chill,
A troubled woman came to our back door
With wrinkled face, half-opened mouth, and eyes
As full of sorrow as the night was full
Of broken clouds, asking to see my mother.
"What is it, Mary?" came from a room upstairs.
"O Kate, come quick, Jane has . . ." and said no more.
Her gaunt and terror-stricken face at times
Disturbs me still. The remnant at the store
In a circle round the big black stove breathed out
A double curse upon the Evangelist,
Gray as the ashes of our disillusion,
And hard as the clinkers lurking in their embers.

Before the Wind

The lazy summer days that melt the air
Over the Northern world as if to share
The bayous of the South with us, and make
Fit restitution for the frozen ache
Of winter's cruelty, began to flow
Full force in early June. Stirred by their glow,

184

Our hibernating spirits battered down
Old mill dams of restraint, flooding the town
With eddies of excitement that converged
To a point on July Fourth, then suddenly merged
Their spindrift to a pattern. The noonday meal
Challenged the women's thought; our pent-up zeal
Was all for games and races, which began
With a parade of "horribles"—each man
And boy and girl the dubious designer
Of take-offs ranging from the initial signer
Of the Great Declaration that released
The noisy festival to the voodoo priest
Of a heathen tribe along the Niger River
The Sunday School books told us of. A shiver
Of joy ran through the crowd when this battalion
Marched on the field. A farmer on a stallion,
Like Cincinnatus risen in the West,
Led the "fantastics" marching two abreast
Straight to the judges' stand where critic eyes
Were waiting to bestow the gaudy prize.

Then followed rowing race, and sculling race,
Running, jumping, wrestling. In a place
Where the ground was smooth beneath tall spruces, bent
The horseshoe pitchers in a tournament
Whose rivalry corralled a voluble crowd
Of onlookers—no banter half so loud
On the spruce point was heard all day. The clang
Of horseshoes striking rods of iron rang
Clear on the field, and cries of "leaner," "ringer,"
Shattered the air till no one but the bringer
Of the welcome "Chowder's ready!" could reclaim
Quoit-pitchers or spectators from the game.

At dinner time a little air arose
Out of the southwest, and the awaited close,
The boat race, was fast getting under way.
Here was the apex of our work and play,
The pinnacle of judgment, courage, skill,
When seaport men confront the breeze's will
In all its treacheries.

                        To three or four
Was generally conceded something more
Than ordinary power—their special luff
Or gybe or tack held something of the stuff
That sets a man apart—the master trait
Most men attribute to the wheel of fate.
Of these Rube Wiley held the palm, his name
Had jumped the boundaries of the state to claim
Glory at Marblehead. One of a crew
Of sailors on a racing yacht, he flew
Into a rage to see his craft behind,
Grew madly bold, went aft, and spoke his mind
To the Captain, got a hearing, took full charge,
Shifted her ballast, trimmed her till her large
Hull quickened through the water, brought her in
The first across the line amid a din
Of bells and sirens—then and there turned down
An offer of big wages that the town
Loved to relate; but Rube preferred the lot
Of independence, and through decades sought
Peace in his hermit-crab-like shell. He found
Life pleasant in a galley where the sound
Of flowing water one could scarcely hear
Rolled music sweeter to his listening ear,
Each night, than Siren's song. Disheveled hair
Of frayed Manila rope gave him the air
Of some old Viking in his Northern lair—
A fierceness that kept people at a distance—
The very people who in many an instance
Growled at his indolent and stubborn turn,
And wasted chances, wishing they could earn
One-half his famous offer.
                        Next to him
Was Swedish Otto, wistful child of whim,
Whose boating skill held scarce a mental notion,
'Twas grounded all on love and sheer emotion.
How often have I seen him contemplate
A coil of rope as if it held the fate
Of his own happiness in every thread,
Then lay it down as one would put to bed
A smiling, healthy baby. He would look

186

Upon the tides as wise men on a book
That gives back things unnoticed or mistook
By casual perusers. He would count
Upon the changes of the moon to mount
The horses of the fog and bring fair weather;
And if they failed, he tugged so at the tether
Of each offending nag, we somehow knew
'Twere better not to cross him. Morning dew,
However slight, revealed to him the clue
Of the day's promise. When he sailed a boat,
He ventured things few other men afloat
Would think of doing in a serious race:
Gamble with tides, run off the course, or place
Himself so far to windward only chance
Or some intuitive trick of clairvoyance
Would bring him in a winner. Yet he won
Hard races and was honored.
                                    Next came one
Who sailed a sloop to lobster pots in all
Varieties of weather from a squall
To calmness that would scarcely chip the top
Of the bay's polished marble. He could stop
Close by a buoy, and allowed it strange
That anyone should miss who knew the range
Of wind and tide. He labored without change
In that one sloop, the *Carrie*, studied her
And studied little else. The ghostly stir
She made when fog mulls drifted in to blur
Her path from trap to trap, and cake mildew
On jib and mainsail, or the gale that blew
So stiff she reared her copper bottom high
Above the waves, spiralling toward the sky,
Were both alike to him. He wore one pair
Of yellow oilskins till he wore them bare,
And a blue denim jumper; people said
He had the same rig on the night he wed.
His moustache settled to a careless droop,
And when the icicles began to loop
Their bases round its fringes, he would look
Like a walrus peering from an island nook.
A primal, one-track mind—his prestige grew

On afternoons when hauling pots was through
By taking on the others for the run
Back from the fishing grounds. John Andrews won
So often half the others shied from him
Unless the breeze just tallied with their whim.

If modesty were favored in a race
Ned Speed on *Onaway* might have claimed first place,
For he was hardly bold enough to let
His boat compete. It stumps one even yet
To say what foiled his shyness when the roll
Of entries was discussed from knoll to knoll.

Artistic shyness that is prone to shun
Whatever things are not superbly done
Lingers in all of us to some degree;
And hence an added grain of sympathy
Lurked in men's tones as they said, "*Onaway*
Will show her heels to some of them today."
Beating to windward was his forte—Ned laid
A boat up closer to the wind and played
Lee bow across the tide with cannier care
Than all the others in our thoroughfare.
Ned was the only one Rube Wiley feared—
Respect for him was heightened by a beard
Whose ends rolled up in silken curls so fine
It gave his face a wistfulness benign.

Of lesser lights I mention only two:
Bold Ellis with two entries loudly blew
His own loud horn. He said that day, "If you
Don't blow your own, there's no one else that will."
"And if you do, there's no one else that will,"
Came quick retort. Himself sailed *Helen U.*
A new black sloop, but *Romp,* an earlier joy,
Was handled this time by his oldest boy
Who carried far more sail than she could swing:
Her bow would bog down in the bay and cling,
Slowing her speed, completely smothering
Whatever chance she had. (This reckless son
Was drowned in her when he was twenty-one.)

188

By two the wind had freshened to a breeze,
And ocean was adorning with white frieze
Long columns of green billows when the call,
"Stand by," was sounded. Seven sloops in all
Were feeling each other out before the run,
Gybing and tacking, waiting for the gun
To send them scurrying across the line.
A shot rings out. "They're off!" and all that's fine
In boat racing is full before us now:
The graceful curve of spray on either bow
Prismed in sunlight; new white sails full spread;
The tightening of the rigging from masthead
To slanting deck; the churning green and white
Beneath the stern; the animated light
In eyes above the tiller, eyes on shore—
All these commingled with the steady pour
Of water over pebbles, wind through boughs
Of spruce and fir conspired to arouse
The village to its loftiest high noon.
The huddling of the boats hid all too soon
From those on shore the fortunes of the race;
Only the experts could precisely trace
Just what was going on: the luff that gave
To *Helen U.* the windward berth, a grave
Infraction of the rules, some said; the way
Queer Otto on his port tack made a play
To speed ebb tide by standing past the rest;
Wiley and Andrews almost fouled abreast
When rounding Garden Island; the fierce squall
That struck so hard on the second leg they all
Pulled down their jibs and lowered peaks as dark
Clouds raced above them toward the outer mark—
All these fine points were not for us; we stood
Spellbound as long as the exciting mood
Was on the crowd; then, "Well, they're off!" which meant
The breathless first intoxication spent,
Parted the group in squadrons. We explored
The grounds for things to do. The judges moored
Beside the starting buoy caught our gaze
And we rowed out to learn of other days
And other races when the rules were lax.

Time lagged, but not for them. The last boat tacks
Around the final marker and the fleet
Squares for the home stretch. Once again men greet
Their neighbors with gay words as if the choice
Each made were special reason to rejoice.
The judges shoo us off, and shade their eyes
Against the dazzling sunlight. Each boat flies
Before the wind, but two are in the lead:
John Andrews sailing *Carrie*, and Ned Speed
In *Onaway*. The others try in vain
New jibs and staysails till the telling strain
Is almost visible on cheeks whose skin
Cannot conceal the torn terrain within—
Each ponders what he might have done to win.

Meanwhile the crowd has eyes for only these
Two in the lead, and hails them as the breeze
Bowls them along before the wind. First one
Is caught by a wave and shunted on the run
A bowsprit length ahead; then comes the other
On a succeeding wave as if to smother
The advantage of the first. The multitude
Watching along the shore are so subdued
Their breathing is a reflex of the rise
And fall of these two sloopboats. Copper skies
Color the final curtain. On the shore
The partial cheering grows to such a roar
When Speed rolls in victorious that the scene
Is like a great convention when the keen
Contenders for high office move to make
The choice unanimous—so in the wake
Of *Onaway* wide billows leaped with glee,
And spruce boughs round the shore reared up to see
The triumph of a son of modesty
Whose joy in winning made still more benign
His beard when he slid first across the line.

PART II

Aunt Cynthia's Story

Aunt Cynthia was one who could remember
When Indians came each year into the cove
To feast on clams and mussels. She well knew
The town held her part Indian: cheekbones
Unduly prominent, a swarthy skin
Brown as the bark of spruces on her path,
Town-shy and village-shy, but bold in the lore
Of pennyroyal, tansy-bags, and mullen—
Feeding us with adventure where the others
Parceled out cookies and said, "Run along!"
Though she protested we had heard it all,
She rarely failed us of our favorite story:

"Sue and I were cleaning house for Sunday—
Sue was scrubbing up the kitchen floor,
And I was tidying the sitting room;
The folks had gone to a daguerreotype saloon
To get Ma's picture taken. All at once
The door flew open and a bearded man
With belted blouse, big boots, and deep sea tan,
Looking for all the world like Captain Kidd,
Sang out, 'Heave ho! don't no one here know me?'
Sue answered, 'No; what do you want round here?'
'If you don't mind, I'll take a drink of water.'
Sue reached for the dipper; he came sidling up
And put his tattooed arm around my waist.
The anchor, wheel, and naked woman showing
On that big arm scared daylights out of me.
I pushed him off with the broom, Sue dropped the dipper,
Water and all, looked him straight in the eye and said,
'Behave yourself! I take it you're a sailor
Out of a schooner in the harbor; we
Have sailors in our family, too; I hope
They know enough to act like decent folks
When they're ashore.'

'Which one are you?' he grinned,
'There's Carrie, Sue, and Cynthia.'
                                    Dumbfounded,
Sue looked him over, head to foot, then said,
'Why, man, can you be Andrew, our big brother
Who went away when we were tucking dolls in?
I don't think anyone but Ma would know you,
And she herself—well, no, perhaps she wouldn't
Be taken in by that sheath knife and beard.'

" 'Of course I'm Andrew, girls—the one that fought
With father on my sixteenth birthday—you
Have heard him tell the story like enough.
He got the better of me that time, though
I swore to his face I'd go and not come back
Till I could throw him down and keep him down,
And here I am.'
                    'Oh, Andrew, don't,' we cried,
'Be hard on father; he is getting old,
Too old for rough and tumble. Come, sit down
And tell us all the places you have been to.'

"He said his first trip on the *Silver Star*
Took him to the South Sea islands where they left
A band of missionaries. There for weeks
He saw the sights among the outer islands,
The palm trees, cocoanuts, and savages.
He sailed to Madagascar after cloves,
Then back to Barcelona loading salt,
And off again to Singapore and Java—
The very names would make you want to go.
He never thought of coming home at all
Except to thrash the old man; now and then
Desire for revenge would come on him,
As squalls come on the sea, and he would wonder
How many minutes it would take to pay
For all the lickings Pa had given him.

"We both kept at him till he yelled, 'Pipe down!'
Then stuck his boots up on the haircloth sofa
And told us of a voyage round Cape Horn

When all the rigging was so tangled up
They had to cut the masts away and steer
With a jury rudder; told how his dearest friend
Washed overboard down in the 'roaring forties'
And swam a long time on the sea; they saw
His yellow oil-coat and sou'wester shining
Against the blue sea for a mile astern;
And when they spied him last an albatross
Was spreading long white wings above his head
And pecking at him. Andrew's face went white
When he told this, as if he saw him still.
They didn't dare to bring the hooker to
For fear she'd open up her seams and founder.
She foundered just the same. They left the pumps,
Abandoned her, and drifted on a raft
For fourteen days; were picked up by a tramp
And carried all the way to San Francisco.
Then sometime later in Perth Amboy harbor
He took a sudden notion to come home
And get that thrashing over once and for all."

Although the outcome was her little secret,
The way Aunt Cynthia told her brother's saga
Set dark clouds stirring in her light blue eyes;
Set breezes loose from all four points of Heaven
To sprinkle every one of us with pollen
That later bloomed on mastheads out to sea.

Storm Visitor

There is a spirit in the northeast storm
That makes the snow twirl on the windowpanes
In a witch's dance to warn people within—
It strikes with anger, lunging out and lifting
Shoulders against the clapboards, banging its head
Under the eaves, wailing a disappointment
That it cannot tear homes from their foundations
And strew them as it strews tall ships at sea.
And something else there is in northeast storms

That tempers and exalts the coastwise man
As noble music purifies and heightens
The soul of him who dwells in its domain;
And when the coast man buttons yellow oilskins
And seeks the shore, ostensibly to tie
His sloop and skiff more firmly, but in truth
To watch white-breasted waves crowd in and jostle,
Hear from the headland the symphonic tones
And overtones that vibrate on the cliff,
The power that drives him there and holds him there
Is the irresistible orchestra of the sea.
Therefore the inmates of a lighted cottage
Hid in a scooped-out ledge close by the shore,
The lintel of whose threshold had been darkened
By the shadow of Death's wings, were not annoyed
When they heard footsteps crunching on the snow
Followed by gentle knocking at the door.

A village Martha who had taken it on her,
As was the custom, to redd up the rooms
And help with kitchen duties, caught her breath
To see a stranger, when she shut the door to,
Instead of some old neighbor dropping in.

"There's nothing going on—this place is lighted
Because a boy is dying of consumption
In an upstairs room—you'll find it pleasanter
At almost any other place in town."
The circle where his hood and red hair met
Made an aureole of snowflakes—a white horseshoe—
And thinking it might bring the house good luck,
She shoved behind his knees the kitchen rocker.

He made no protest, spoke no word, but listened
As if he heard the sound of sailors crying
On shipwrecked schooners in the blinding bay.
The sorrow-blinded father looked at him
As one grief-laden shipmate to another,
And fearing his reception had been cool,
Put out the hand of welcome while explaining,
"We cannot do much for you here tonight;

194

But you are welcome to the little we have,
So make yourself at home."
                                    The stranger looked
Deep in the father's eyes, and laid his hand
Upon the mother's arm, for silently
She, too, was drawn and held by sympathy
Longer than she had planned, from the upstairs room.
The stranger sat there till the room grew chilly,
Then found the woodpile in a little lean-to—
A hillock of green alders that bespoke
A house of poverty. He lugged it in,
Armful by armful, placed it in the oven
And baked it dry, as dwellers on the coast
Had done for years and years. The alders' fragrance
Is unlike any other—some believe
The reed they smote our Lord with was of alder,
And when they lashed it out, he touched and blessed it,
Anointing it with incense that has held
Its tang for centuries. Those who have known
The aroma when the oven door is opened
Remember pungent anodyne for grief
Of secular dimension. But the way
He touched the alders and suffused the rooms
With balmy perfume on that gusty night
Went far beyond the secular—it calmed
And comforted a sorrowing house of death.

All night he went from room to room and filled
The place with waves of fragrance. His large eyes
Conveyed a sympathy that reached across
The gulf no bridge of words can ever span,
However arched and buttressed. All within
Were calmed as if he issued from the storm
To drive the greater storm of grief away.
He seemed the peace at the center of all storms—
The fourth who stood beside the Hebrew worthies
In the burning fiery furnace, and the third
On that Emmaus walk with Cleopas
And his companion whose renewed hearts burned
Within them as they talked beside the way.
He disappeared before the break of dawn,

Though no one saw him go. The father asked
When he came down, "Who was the stranger with us?"

"He didn't tell his name," the woman answered,
"Or say where he was from. At first I thought
He must be someone off a ship—then knew
That could not happen in a big northeaster.
I wondered all night long just who he was,
He kept the place so warm, and almost cheerful,
In spite of everything. Is Enoch better?"

"We trust he is," the stricken father faltered,
Then pausing, looked out on the wave-still ocean;
"I felt like you about that man, and she . . ."
He pointed to the chamber overhead
Where the mother wept beside her death-cold son.

Captain Rivers

When Captain Rivers walked the village street,
After a voyage in the China trade
Or up the Nile, he somehow smote the air
With the same gradual plunge his full-rigged ship
Employed to smite the barriers of waves
On oceans whose mere names brought smell of spice
And clink of gold to those who stayed at home.
Perhaps the velvet corduroys he wore,
The braid of blue on his Prince Albert coat,
The tall black stovepipe hat and mammoth watch chain
Enhanced the magic of his name beyond
The names of other masters. But one more
Topgallant sail in his full-rigged equipment
Endeared him to the mothers of the town
Beyond all these, beyond the serious whiskers
Of sisal and burnt ochre that enwrapped
His visage in persuasive dignity—
A reverence for the claims of true religion.
On Sunday mornings when he walked to church
The entire town gave heed; his Congress shoes

Squeaked his arrival and processional
Until he docked in the front and center pew
Close by the pulpit, and when he sat down
Some little boys concluded God himself
Had come to quicken and enlarge the hour.
Fond mothers mused, "If my boy goes to sea,"
(And what lad then refused the adventurous call?)
"I hope he signs to go with Captain Rivers."

The service over, he would choose a few
To come on board that afternoon for tea,
And there when village conversation turned,
As it invariably was wont to turn,
To the sermon of the morning, he would say,
"On *this* ship we have services each Sunday."

On one such Sunday when a timid mother
Whose winter had been spent persuading John,
Her only son, that sailor life was hardship—
Salt horse unfit to eat, and foreign tongues
He could not hope to speak—went slowly home
Weak and uncertain in her course, the boy,
Sensing her mood of insecurity,
Put feelers out once more for voyaging,
And drew from her a qualified assent,
"I know your feelings, John, and if you must
Take one sea voyage, will you promise me
That you will only go with Captain Rivers?"

The day he left was like a launching day:
An air of gaiety blew round the dock
Where resinous scent of pine and tarry rigging
Inspired the old with Orient memories,
The young with visions of enchanting ports
Reached only through this cordage and this pine.
A tugboat whistled, and past waving arms
And fluttering handkerchiefs and loud good-byes
Convoyed the black hulk to the harbor's mouth
Where she was swallowed up. The lonely mother,
Shadows playing on her face like ripples
Along the great ship's dark and shadowy lee,

Culled one small grain of comfort all that night,
"This Captain Rivers is a man of prayer
With services each week—what else could urge
His ship along more swiftly, better bring
His priceless human cargo safely home?"

But Captain Rivers having once put off
His ministerial coat and stovepipe hat
Turned treacherous as tide rip. When the mate's
"Aloft and shorten sail" rang out in sharp
Staccato for the first time, and John lingered
A bit behind the rest, the Captain ran
Swinging a lanyard, bellowing, "Don't let me
See you again the last one in the rigging—
You landlubber, take this." John scampered skyward,
Dodged the lash, and dared no more look back
Than he would face the Devil; but beneath
His right arm caught a glimpse of his commander,
As artists catch a fresh view of old landscape,
And had no doubt that Satan himself had come
On this unlucky voyage billeting
His spirit in the Captain's altered face.
With right hand clutched against his old horse pistol,
Threatening to put the whole damned crew in irons,
With marlinspike, belaying pin, and lanyard,
He drove the men like slaves about the deck,
Till John heard mutterings of mutiny,
And caught himself upsurging in its wake.

Meanwhile his mother read the shipping news
Crowding the New York *Herald*—tiny scraps,
So unexpanded, yet so full of meaning,
Like telltale driftwood on a morning sea—
Till one forenoon a scrap more intimate
Drifted into her home from San Francisco.
The expected document seemed all too short,
But there stood his handwriting plain before her
And her eyes glowed. *"Dear Mother, Captain Rivers
Is not the man we thought he was."* Just this,
And nothing more. And though the mother wept
And moaned all night that there was nothing more,

The town secreted every syllable
Deep in the salty archives of its heart.

Lem Baker

Lem Baker watched his comrades stroll down street
With interwoven arms and hands on shoulders,
Yet walked himself alone. On festive days
When banking brush was burning, or a well
Just dug was yielding up its crystal gusher
For the first time, while others danced around,
Saluting neighbors, hailing fellow revelers
In helter-skelter glee, Lem drew apart,
And drew still more apart if they but tried
To grasp his hand in their hilarity.
He blamed himself for his too much aloofness,
And half resolved at times to enter in
Wholeheartedly when some new celebration
Gave him the chance. But each new opening found him
More and more like the hermit crabs that lay
Listening in the mud below the fishhouse
For sound of rubber boots.
                                        No previous crisis
In all his thirty years could quite approach
The one confronting him that August morning,
After the big revival of the Eighties,
Calling the village to confess, repent,
And be baptized in Christ. Shy Lem "came out"
Along with other converts of that year,
And made known his resolve to be baptized.
But when the time came for the sacred rite,
The grace of God itself was not enough
To overcome the fear of touch and pressure
On his too shrinking body. There he stood,
And there the evangelist reached out willing arms
Ready to hold and plunge him in the tide—
Yet Lem drew back. The preacher waded up
And reached out arms once more, and yet once more

Lem, like a startled heron, moved away.
By this time people on the shore were poking
Their fingers in each other's ribs and starting
Conniption antics that annoyed the preacher.
He swept the crowd with an appraising eye,
And hurriedly whispered something reassuring;
But Lem, still unpersuaded, hurled an answer
Loud enough for everyone to hear—
*"Now, parson, you just say the blessed words,
And I'll be off and under like a porpoise."*

Revelation

Jane Wiley, with four stricken sons,
Cursed God when the first two went,
But a third near death brought her knees to earth,
Her eyes to the firmament.

By the kitchen door, the child in her arms,
The first warm night of spring,
She prayed, "O Lord, let fall some sign
To ease my suffering."

Her heart, pursued through a darkling wood,
Made her woman's will more strong
To tear the mask from the face of Death
That had shadowed her path too long.

She looked toward the east when, silent, there rose
A billowy bubble of light
Floating, shimmering over the marsh—
A will-o'-the-wisp in the night.

Though its girth was small as the child's toy ball,
Its glow, of softer hue
Than the pearliest tints on the tide, was good
Saint Elmo lighting her through

Her blackest hour. The blaze that shone
Near Damascus ages ago
Was a signal from Heaven to Saul no more
Than this will-o'-the-wisp's mild glow

To a frightened mother holding her breath
By the marsh, intent to find
A lantern to light the feet of Death
Through the marshes of her mind.

To a Pessimist

There are green trees with us still,
And ever shifting sunrises to thrill
Awakening birds and men; there is the sea
In calm or tempest whose immensity
Can fill our deeper needs if we but lean
And hearken to her song; there are the mountains
Lifting their shaggy cones toward heaven's fountains
Of many a shape and size; and lifting, too,
Man's spirit upward toward the ascending blue
To which all trees and birds and ocean waves aspire.
There is the friend
Whom you can count on to the very end
Of your long trek and his; the patient wife
Who holds you dearer than her own dear life;
The merry girl and pioneering boy
She had with you, and, trailing these, the free
Wave-bubbling laughter of the babe whose glee
Can pierce your dullest hour with sudden joy,
Filling the home with raggle-taggle mirth.
And when you reckon what the trek was worth,
And lay aside your pack reluctantly,
There are the waiting arms of mother earth—
The earth that gave you mountains, forest, ocean,
Friends, children, lovers—hers the last devotion,
For you belong to her. Oh, go in trust
That through the cycling years from dust to dust
The mettle of your spirit is of such

Ingredients tempered by her saltier touch
The stuff of heaven in you can break the clay
To spring as fresh as flowers on Easter day.

Brad's Daughter

A tea rose blooming 'mid calendulas,
We loved the eagerness of Caroline,
Brightening the village street, raising the question
How one such flower could bloom from two such stalks
As hard-shelled Brad and Her Indifference,
His meekly echoing wife. Decisions were
His province—even those that other men
Leave to the kitchen he carried to the barn
And settled while his horses chomped their hay
And cattle ruminated in their stanchions.
Finalities became this man who built
Well curbs of granite that would last forever,
Who built his granite faith upon the Word,
Unmixed with symbol or elaboration,
Faith that enabled his gigantic frame
To pulverize Maine rock to fertile field.

Trying enough to delicate Caroline
The drab ménage itself, without the hard
Unyielding piety her father made
The central beam and girder of his life—
Piety that wrought on her like kapok poison,
A blight that failed to heal, which country doctors
Could neither diagnose nor treat—till one,
A clean-cut novice, young, and fresh from Harvard,
Told her to go to Boston, there entrust
Her nerve-torn spirit to a master healer
Whom he revered.
                        "It's not for me to say;
My father must decide."
                        Brad shook his head,
Complained about the long and arduous trip,

About the fees great doctors would require,
Though he was thriftier than most and need
Have had few wrenchings here. Reluctantly
(The tea rose petals withering till the neighbors
Winced at the gathering blight), he finally said,
"Pack up your dunnage, Caroline, and go."

Surprised and pleased to find the great man simple,
She turned her petals toward him, eager to find
In him a healing for her withering shoots:
Told of her father's farm, his Baptist faith
That drove them all to sit through tedious sermons,
And testify at Thursday evening meetings—
(This latter chore her special detestation,
For she was timid as a jewelweed pod
Touched by a clumsy and determined hand)—
Told him about her girlhood reveries,
Her longing for a life where lips were closed
In gentleness, not snapped in turtle fashion
Till some household command were carried out.
Still more surprised was she at telling him
These things that long lay festering in her heart.

We never knew just why a Science healer
Came to her bedside in the hospital
(We half-suspected the great man himself)
And told her of a faith, a Christian faith,
That was not drab nor dour, but aglow
With upward-streaming sunshine, beauty, cheer—
A faith that shone among the other creeds
Like tea rose blooms amid calendulas,
Which she at once embraced. We only knew
The whispering that passed from lip to lip
Of Caroline turned Scientist, enough
To shake our village on its rock foundations
As whirlwinds shook the Cities of the Plain.
It set her father walking through the pasture,
Set neighbors wondering what he would do.
They saw the turtle jaw snap hard and harder
And hold on tighter than before; they saw

Him shake his graying head from side to side,
And heard him utter somber imprecations
Half-audibly between his spreading teeth.
His wife grew frightened when he went out walking
For hours after midnight through ploughed fields,
Praying by high stone walls. At last it seemed
A light had come to guide him, and relief
That he had kept his sanity relaxed
The tension tightening every doweled timber
That held the house together. Christmas brought
A telegram in buoyant, joyous phrases
Saying that Caroline was coming home,
And wanted all to meet her at the station.
Her brother was the only one to go.
He drove her just at nightfall up the lane—
A cold December nightfall—all the stars
In their familiar places shining clear
Filled her with added joy: the Pleiades
Dancing out of the east over the sea;
Old Taurus risen below them golden clear
Darting a greeting just above the woodshed.
Laughing, she raised her hand to him and turned
To meet a different Taurus in the doorway.

The tragic, righteous figure of her father
Pointing his hard forefinger like a pistol
Straight at her face, unloosed his stored-up wrath
Like some old patriarch offering sacrifice:
"You have disowned your father, Caroline,
Yes, more than that, disowned the one true God
I and your mother worship. You have disowned
Your Baptist faith, your people, and gone whoring
After false gods. The Word of God tells me
To cast you out. Now go! And never again
Set foot across my threshold." They all stood
Searching each other's faces for an answer,
Trembling with indecision. Long, too long
Had he decided for them. Caroline,
Herself the calmest, looked upon them all,
Bowed down with grief, and yet afraid to speak,

204

Cowed by the fervor of a son of Calvin,
True to the darkness which he called his light,
Who let no wall of partition come between
His unrelaxing conscience and his God.

Malachi Bascom

Malachi Bascom scoured the sea
In a Bedford whaler of 'fifty-three;
Rose to be captain, settled down
After his beard had lost its brown,
In the picture-book New England town
He knew by heart. He wanted rest,
But, anchored, found himself distressed
That New York City and the West
Should filch the young ones from his nest;
While a murkier West, bereft of brine,
Had curtained his good wife Caroline.

His sky of health turned black with rain
When he found the quiet life of Maine
Packed no such hygienic wallop
As a full-rigged ship on a Gulf Stream gallop.
Distress to desperation grew,
So the Captain married off anew—
This time to a stout and crafty widow
Whose previous figure cast a shadow
Of generous girth enough; but now,
The last care lifted from her brow,
She felt herself at ease to batten
On precious sweets. Did that girl fatten!

She waxed so roundly corpulent
(Though quite aside from her intent)
That when she swayed toward the dinner table
Puffing as hard as the wolf in the fable,
The Captain, white with anger, thought,

"I'll find some means to fetch up taut
This *whewing* habit of the wife,"
So, running true to whaler life,
Whenever her great bosom rose,
He squared to a majestic pose,
And boomed a long-drawn "Arrr-she-blows!"

The Ballad of the Gunning Rock

A Coast Guard watchman at sunrise stared
On the blue and gold of the sea,
Dotted with half-tide rocks that shared
The ocean's treachery.

The half-tide ledges that morning lay
Like a gentle herd of cows
Come up from the ocean to graze in the bay:
There was scarcely a ripple to rouse

Bulls in the herd, though one roared loud
Where his captain and messmates two
Were banging at coots—his brother proud
Of a place in the favored crew.

The envious watchman turned away
With a sigh which asked why some
Spin out their years like a holiday—
And straightway started to hum

A deep-sea chanty; turned again
Toward the rock where his brother gunned:
The dory was floating away, and the men
Had vanished! Bewildered, stunned,

And too unsettled to ring or hail,
He ran to the station for aid,
Babbling such a harrowing tale
The crustiest there were afraid.

Though fear was on them that heard him speak,
They launched the lifeboat, sped
To the gunning rock—now mild and meek
As a great dun cow well fed.

They towed the dory home, but found
No trace of the men; they dragged
With grapplings night and day around
That rock. A fortnight lagged

Before the bodies rose on the tide,
For no east wind was found
To warp the sea's dark wall aside
And show how the men were drowned.

At the village store on winter eves
Some ponder what befell
This luckless trio: one believes
The Devil out of Hell

Appeared upon that ledge—they shook
And crumpled at his nod;
Another holds they caught one look
At the luminous face of God.

But neither we nor their wives could find
(Nor shall till Judgment Day)
What angel or demon struck them blind
And toppled them into the bay.

Fred Rowley

Spruce buds and needles and dead broken twigs
Now fill the body of this scow where once
Fred Rowley lived to close a life of shame.
The bayberry bushes and wild pear trees lean
Over the weather-warped decaying sides,
Spilling their fragrance with the selfsame joy

And generosity their brothers reeve
About the homes of simple fisher folk
Whose going out and coming in are patterned
By tides that stir the pebbles on their shores.

In early years Fred's story varied little
From that of other men along the coast:
Good with a pair of oars, quick and resourceful
Handling a sailboat in deceitful weather,
Skillful in fitting out a scow like this,
That carried brush for building herring weirs,
Birch brush and stakes torn yearly from these hills.
Like most of us he took the trip to sea
In a black-hulled fore-and-after with white sails,
And smelled green coffee piled on Southern docks,
And heard the Negroes singing at their labor.
Like most of us he soon forsook his berth
In cooped-up forecastles and settled down
Where he could stretch himself in glowing freedom—
Could paddle round with codfish line and gun,
And so combine the casual ways of nomads,
Whose tug is never absent from us long,
With those of squatters who turn up new soil
And watch new gardens ripening to the harvest.
More pointedly than others he preferred
The ways of separation, and more marked
Than that of others was his negligence
Toward weeds that choked the garden. Never quite
Like other settlers had he made the break
Out of the hunting, fishing, trapping stage
Of planetary life: no man around
Could sail a boat like Fred, or trip an old-squaw
With such unerring skill—he kept his gun
Bright as a piece of newly minted silver,
Loaded the shells himself, and brought in birds
That had small trouble keeping out of range
Of other hunters—thus we often wondered
What skill alive in him had died in us.

These birds of varied plumage he would mount
In many a striking pose—here a hawk

Gathering his agile body for a plunge
In channel water; there a mammoth heron
Standing like the statue of an ibis;
Down on the floor an enormous snake
Luring a lovely goldfinch into darkness.
One evening hard beset by weariness
He put a touch of arsenic to his tongue
And felt revived. The act grew to a habit,
Large and larger grew the amounts he needed,
Till all at once it seemed his separation
Had been perfected by the estranging drug.
From that time on he moved more like a deer
That skirts the fringes of the hills, and stands
Gazing at evening over lonely shores,
Than like a human being with his kind.
His skill and wisdom in all nature lore
Became a village legend—that he knew
Unerringly the curious names and ways
Of birds, crustaceans, and vagrant flowers
Confounded village folk that knew them not.
They marveled at his prowess: when a weir man
Beheld at dawn trapped in his flood-tide pound
A giant leatherback turtle never seen
Before in northern bays, and watched in fear
The ease with which it ripped the seine, he sent
Post haste for Fred, who soon subdued the monster,
Mounted its leather hide, and charged a fee
From all the curious hundreds who came hither
To view the creature—hundreds who left to spread
Further the boundaries of the growing legend;
And when a fisherman was drowned, and surfmen
Equipped for dragging failed to find the body,
The village, as one man, called out for Fred,
Whose grappling iron caught the unlucky victim,
And with it dragged Fred's fame to loftier heights.

His wife who loved good fellowship was driven
To be herself a creature of the wild.
At times she half-rebelled and made him go
Sit out the evening with a sister living
Across a stretch of woods a mile away.

He cherished quiet hours with his birds,
His arsenic, and his taxidermist dreams,
And went against his wishes. When she told
How much she craved companionship and talk
Of neighborhood amenities that brought
Boredom to him, he trailed her like a schoolboy
Who hates the jangling school bell calling him in.
He took his gun along for company;
His hand upon the gunstock felt a touch
Of happiness sweeter than any touch
That she could bring to bear upon his hand.
He hoped to meet a lucifee and watch
Bright eyes peer out behind a dark spruce bole,
Or hear the wild geese honking overhead
And shoot into the darkness at their cry.

One night his protests grew more voluble,
For he was working on a large white heron,
The pride of his collection—and he growled
At any interruption; but she too
Was stuffed with stubbornness, and made a stand
To have her fancies catered to. In anger
He dropped the bird, picked up his gun, and went,
The wrath within him mounting every hour,
Nourished considerably by one large nip
He took before he left. In sullen silence
He listened to the small talk, or pretended
That he was listening—his mind was spinning,
As a hummingbird spins poised above white lilacs,
Spinning round that white bird in the parlor,
Knowing it never would be mounted quite
As it should be—for this untoward intrusion;
And on the journey home a rage beset him
That laid his wife next day in the shade-drawn parlor
Beside the unfinished masterpiece that stood
In velvet moss, a sharp knife in its bosom.

Next morning dawned the Sabbath; sunlight gleamed
Over the rocks and through the green spruce boughs
As if to clarify the ghastly news

Now shadowing the village. No event
In all its previous history had held
Import so grave as this. The muddy roads
Were lined with carriages and wagons seeking
A lonely clump of spruce where birds and rabbits
Held undisputed sway the previous Sunday.
The village felt strange pride in its importance,
And we all joined the crowd that swept toward Rowley's.
Fred walked himself beside the coroner
And led our curious feet through tall spar timber
Till he came to a fallen tree across a path—
There stopped and pointed out where he put down
The gun to help her over. He described
How when he picked it up, the hammer caught
Across a jagged limb, drew back, discharging
Buckshot in the woman's heart and lungs,
Killing her instantly. Fred's pallid face,
A pallor heightened by the whitening drug,
That moment drew a sigh of sympathy
From everyone except the coroner.
Back to the house we went, where hundreds stood
Waiting a glimpse of him whose lawless deed
Set him apart. They somehow looked to see
The brand of Cain marked visibly on his brow.
No man we knew had shunned the gaze of men
With half the zeal of Fred, yet there he stood,
Pain tearing at his face; but who could tell
Whether his spirit's loathing of the mob
Or grief for his dead wife was at the root
Of this phrenetic terror? In he went
And closed the door behind him—whereupon
The coroner drew the neighbors dwelling near
A little way apart and said, "If you
Who know this man and live here entertain
Suspicion of foul play, speak now, and I
Will bring the case before the next Grand Jury
When it convenes." Some neighbors entertained
Suspicion of naught else except foul play,
But not one word against him would they utter
For some New England reason of their own.

A fortnight later Rowley woke to find
A message fastened to his kitchen doorknob
Signed by these selfsame noncommittal neighbors,
"You are hereby commanded to get out,
Or we will strip your gear, and make your life
Miserable in every way we can."
Thus Fred became a Maine coast Ishmael,
Sold at a sacrifice his rare collection,
His boats and gear, and furtively moved away.
A few took pity on him as he stood
Waiting the stage's coming; he appeared
That morning like a lost soul preyed upon
Continually by "the worm that dieth not."
His piercing ice-blue eyes surveyed the ground
As if he studied insects none of us
Was keen enough to see. His light brown hair
Whose fringes fell below his brown cloth cap
Did little to alleviate the sharp
Drawn look on his emaciated face
That rose above emaciated shoulders
Drooping in contemplation of his lot.
Kind words of sympathy brought nothing more
Than "Yes" or "No" or a turning of the shoulder
Away from him that spoke, as if attention
Were salt upon the sore of his departure.
He sat alone upon the back seat looking
The image of dejection—one of those
Sad creatures Giotto might have used to deepen
His darkly haunting "Burial of Jesus."

Word from Down East the next spring startled us
With tidings of a second Rowley marriage,
To a widow whose grown sons were in the West.
He brought his new wife to a neighboring town,
Causing the doubtful shake of many a head.
The joy was not for long of this new marriage:
Their second wedded year had scarce begun
When rumor whispered that he left his bed
And stretched a cod line tight across the stairs,
Then called on her to go and fetch some pills

Which he was taking for the exacting habit.
'Tis said she tripped across the line and toppled
Headlong down the rickety flight of stairs,
Whereupon he gathered up the cord and ran
To a nearby house bidding them call a doctor.
She lived a week, and in that week made known
The woes she had endured from this drug-ridden
Bluebeard of the coast whose aberrations
Were quite as much a mystery to him
As they could be to any one of us.

After his second wife had snapped the warp
That held her hovering between life and death,
He found himself the object of a crew
Of meddling, curious people, one of them
The county attorney with a list of questions
That Fred was loath to answer. When he left
Fred made a sharp resolve to quit the coast.
He sold his gear once more and moved away
To clean Ontario's low-lying shores,
Purchased a birch canoe of Indians,
An outfit such as northern trappers carry
Across hard portages before the snow
And ice shut down all winter transportation
Save that on foot. He did not need to learn
The ways of Indians, for the primitive
Design of life was his from childhood up.

Far from drugs and drugstores in the north,
He tended traps and cured his numerous pelts,
And lived a busy winter unmolested
By anything more curious than the mink,
The beaver, and the otter making tracks
About his lean-to in the powdery snow.
When spring arrived he paddled down the river
And over lakes to town and sold his furs,
Deciding he had found an anodyne
For the long illness of his previous life.
He paddled over new lakes all that summer
Pursuing muskellunge and speckled trout,

And making plans for trapping in the fall.
One afternoon he set his tent up early
That he might keep the ruddy hours of evening
Uninterrupted for lake trout. The wind
Blew him away from his well-chosen campground
And down the "arm" he went with rod and reel.
The paddle back was longer than he reckoned,
But high cliffs on the right, and on the left
A yellow moon for company, gave him strength
To compensate the hazard of head wind
That kicked up ripples on the darkening lake.
For two bright hours he gloried in the challenge
Of rough wind on his face, but steady watching
Of rippling water under shadowy cliffs
So worked upon his fancy that he saw
The ripples just ahead and on his right
Transform themselves from waves to animals
Cavorting on the lake for his delight—
As creatures of the early world paraded
Before grandfather Adam to receive
His benediction and a christening name.
The beaver, mink, and otter he had trapped
The previous winter now came back to life,
Leaping across each other's backs and under
Each other's curious legs and shadowy tails.
Out of the quaint procession of the creatures
He had been living with appeared a camel,
Hauling a wagonload of otter pelts;
And just behind a tiny elephant
Dragging a circus van of mink and beaver.
The elephant and all the other creatures
Were black as ebony, and when Fred dared
Let go the fascination of the antics
These creatures were enacting underneath
The darkening shadow of that giant cliff
Lit by an orange moon, he chid himself
For holding out so long, and went to bed
To dream of blood that dripped from a red moon
Into his mouth, and woke in fear next day,
Resolving to preserve his sanity
By heading for his native coast once more.

Returning quietly, he fed his hope
Of one more marriage on a journal filled
With matrimonial advertising bait
For hungry men. He scanned the willing prospects
In this seductive sheet, and hit on one
Whose only drawback was a trivial debt
Which she required her suitor to discharge
Before she dared come on. Her looks beguiled
His palpitating heart as he composed
A letter to her full of flourishes
In old Spencerian penmanship that struck
Romantic chords in her neglected breast.
He paid the debt and cleaned as best he could
His cabin by the sea, and watched impatiently
Each mail stage that rolled in. At length the woman
Was driven to his door; and they were wed.
She asked at once for household furnishings
Better than those his world had ever known.
At first he humored her extravagance
And purchased freely, but the day arrived
When he put down his foot, saying, "I'll pay
For no more foolishness, so be content
From this time on with what I can afford."
She saw him buying things that he required
To stuff his specimens and slake his craving,
And soon rebelled. Dissension rocked the hut,
Till he withdrew the small amounts he gave her,
And she in desperation and starvation
Sought refuge in the poorhouse. He sold out
His furnishings to thrifty neighbors, sold
The hut itself, and came for sanctuary
To this abandoned scow here on the beach;
Here bought a green, decrepit lobster wherry,
And set just traps enough to keep himself
From joining her. Distinctly I remember
The quaver in his voice when he gave warning
That I must not tell people he was making
Enough to keep the two of them. At last
He grew so feeble he could not haul one
More lobster pot, or catch the bait he needed;
And found himself too broken to protest

Reunion with her in the village poorhouse
Where he to this day waits indifferently
The coming of the scow that ferries men
Across the fog-encumbered straits of Death.

The Fate of the Royal Tar
(As Told by an Old Settler)

"Come to the wharf and you shall see
The world's most wonderful menagerie—
Elephants from Africa, lions, too,
And the greatest marsupial kangaroo
Fresh from Auster-a-li-a; wart hogs, ounces,
And double-humped camels with fringy flounces.
Don't miss the snakes and boa constrictors,
Slaves from the South and Roman lictors
Dressed as they were in Caesar's day;
And a uniformed band from Paraguay,
With the latest tunes of the U. S. A.
For twenty-five cents you can see it all."

Who could resist such a wonderful call?
Not we who were nourished from year to year
On Noah's Ark, why, the Ark was here!
And some who had scruples when Barnum's tent
Was pitched by the depot (of course, they went
To welcome it in at the flick of dawn)
Had no such qualms at this great hulk drawn
Up to the wharf—there was sanction wise
In Holy Writ for this enterprise.
They even expected, so well they knew
The tale, that the monsters, two by two,
Would strut as they did for Noah's crew.

I see her now as a squalid craft
Crowded with animals fore and aft,
With smelly animals pacing their cages,
Venting their wrath in various rages—

See her all too clear; but then my eyes,
Tinctured with youth's prismatic dyes,
Saw the red plush cabin, a gallery grand,
Like a room in the mansions of the Promised Land.
And the chandelier hanging, a ruby chalice,
Would have graced a hall in the Shushan palace.
The snake-charmer standing, golden-haired and tall,
Was Eve in the Garden just before the Fall;
And the blindfolded wizard, adding reams on reams,
Was Joseph in Egypt unraveling dreams.
The strong man was Samson, and the lion-tamer shone
Like Daniel in the dungeon of Babylon.

We stood on the wharf when she sailed away
Out of the harbor kicking up spray.
Leaving a wake of white at her stern
That bubbled toward the dock like butter in a churn.
We heard the animals' dwindling groans,
Saw red-coated Negroes rolling the bones;
And the Stars and Stripes on the autumn air
Turned the Hebrew legends to a Down East fair.
The day being over I heaved a sigh
To know such glories could be born and die.

The boys of Vinalhaven, where the next stop came,
Saw the marvels we had witnessed, and, O grief too hard
        to name,
Saw the wonder ship of ocean going up in flame.
The story rose and widened, in a fortnight grew
To Biblical proportions. Was there ever such a crew?
The animal-trainers set their charges free,
And shoved them off the deck in the cold Maine sea.
The captain on the poop, ringed round with fire,
Yelled orders in vain, for a thousand times higher
Were the roars and groans of the beasts that rolled
In the fiery furnace of that vessel's hold.
A Negro risked his life for a pony he fed;
A dog-trainer labored till he singed his head;
The keeper of a llama that had just given birth
To a white baby llama on a handful of earth
Took the helpless thing ashore on the last boat freed,

But the mother beast was lost in that wild stampede.
These three were labeled on their very next show
As Shadrach, Meshach, and Abednego.

And some in that furnace would never feel
The up-and-down fortunes of another keel;
But those who came through told the weirdest tale
Of that blazing night. Our cheeks went pale
To hear how the animals swam, though spent,
Round that ball of fire, like moths intent
On a lighted lamp; how the herring, too,
In the harbor leaped toward the flame and flew
Till they hit the deck; how the snakes' dark skin
Turned iridescent as a minnow's fin;
And the snakes' green eyes on the purple sea
Were emeralds bedded in porphyry.
Of the beasts set free the bulk went down
By the burning ship, but a new renown
Was in wait for the few that swam ashore.
To hear a lordly lion roar
On an island nub was a thing to boast
For boys of this quiet northern coast:
But there one stood the color of sand
In the cove beside him, guarding the land.
A chestnut stallion was seen next day
On a half-tide rock far out in the bay;
And the stories of snakes in the bushes grew
Till the blackberries rotted on the vines. All through
The island ran shudders, but they really seemed slight
Compared to the jungle of our dreams at night.

In one wild nightmare I was chopping up a snake
When a lion swam toward me on the burning lake;
I tried hard to run, but heard the pound, pound
Of forty-'leven elephants beating up the ground,
Tearing through the spruces; on the leader sat
A little baby llama in a red plush hat.
A tiger just above me in an island spruce
Made a leap for the llama, his jaws dripping juice.
He wriggled on his belly to eat me up
When an orangoutang with a moustache cup

218

Full of blood, and a razor, said, "Come, shave me,
Or pizzle-end-up in the bottom of the sea
You go!" In a jiffy he put me on a plank
And shoved me in the water where I shivered and sank
Till my back hit a spike on the *Royal Tar*'s rail
And woke me up; I could still feel the nail
In my back when I woke—some kink, I guess,
But wasn't I happy to be out of that mess!

One year later walking up the hill
Folks of Vinalhaven had a brand-new thrill—
For out on the spot where the *Royal Tar* lay
Red flames shot up, then faded away.
They looked at one another, "Did you? And you?
See that flame take shape? Then it must be true."
They remembered and believed, and for many a year
On that autumn night a crowd would appear
Looking out toward Eggemoggin Reach to behold
The *Royal Tar* rising in a circle of gold.
And some saw a sign that the flood of Noah's warning
Would yield to fire on the Judgment Morning.
But other folks went to bask in the glow
Of the one great horror they would ever know.

PART III

The 100% American

"You take the road to Moscow;
And you the road to Rome;
And should you, one or both, turn back,
Look for me here at home
Pondering a new road
By the slope of a Western sea,
That ends where man may bide his span
In glorious anarchy."

Cove at High Water

Green is the cove, the fresh green shade
Of alders when the sun is clear;
And green the spruce-tree branches laid
Over the cove that lean and peer
On dark green pollock—fish that steer
In silent grace round jade-green ledges;
And golden green the cut-grass, dear
To frightened minnows. Morning pledges
Of loyalty to this green spot
Gay warblers pour in notes that rest
On me like gray-green moss inwrought
To ease this granite bowlder's breast.
O emerald nook of coolness, hear
My thanks for this green atmosphere.

There Is an Hour at Evening

There is an hour at evening on the sea
When the white yacht of day is not yet gone,
And the black barge of night is coming on,
That never fails to leave its wake in me:
The mingled blacks and grays that cannot free
Their strands to one clear pattern; the weird chill
Of nightfall with its shuddering breeze; the spill
Of shadows on the bay's periphery—
These awe me standing on a seaside bank;
But on a sloop at anchor as she rides
Silently in the harbor, a thin plank
The only sheath between me and the tides,
I feel Eternity has snubbed the barque
Of Time caught hurrying onward toward the dark.

The Lost Generation

A parent-centered home was ours from birth;
We learned the Ten Commandments word for word;
A few were meaningless, and none was worth
The hours we wrestled with them—we preferred—
What we preferred meant less than winds that blew
Out of the south on Sunday. How absurd
Would "Let's go Sunday sailing!" bristle through
The hirsute ears of that Arminian crew!

A children-centered home is ours to bear;
The Fifth Commandment, light as cascade foam,
Brushes their minds, then filtrates into air;
While we, like senators of ancient Rome,
Are driven to dark corners by the din
Of swaggering Barbarians—mere home
Their base of exploitation; mention Sin,
Salvation, or Damnation, and they grin.

And we, poor we, who never held the reins,
Know nothing of command, let tyrants rule,
Like Stalin, Mussolini, Hitler—banes
To all free spirits; our lost tribe a tool—
A sorry tool for ruthless men to wield;
Down through the ages will the taunt of "Fool"
Be heaped on us who never held the field,
Condemned for life to bear the yoke and yield.

Smoky Southwester

The sun peers dimly through smoke-colored clouds
That scud into the north where gathering haze
Softens the distant islands and enshrouds
The ruby cliffs in undulating grays.
The surge of ocean echoing through the air
Reverberates like intonations heard

In Caribbean conch-shell windings where
The groove retains the untranslated word.
The haze and smoke above this northern tide
Rouse me on such a day: the unquiet trees
And tremulous coves hold something they would hide—
Something that touches on the mysteries
Of life and death—vague adumbrations far
Beyond the smoke and haze of what we are.

High-Water Slack

On late June days I love to stand and see
The tide come in and cover reef and rock,
Ruffle the sand as breezes ruffle a tree
And waken it from silence; round the dock
Flounders glide in and boys with bamboo poles
Are there to greet them; all the village lifts
In valence with the sea, and nature rolls
Up to a higher level. Signal shifts
Await us when the tide no longer floods:
Fish end their biting, earth goes strangely still;
The halting mood intimidates the woods,
Nothing is heard except the brooklet's rill—
The sea stands like the moon in Ajalon,
Before the devastating ebb comes on.

To

The taste of your lips
Is like the tang of the air
On the curved sea beach
The morning after a storm,
When the bosom of the cove
In its palpitant rise and fall
Bears on its grape-green surface
Rolling redundance of light.

222

Wave after wave after wave
Comes flinging its fullness of spray,
Churning the sea as brown
As the tan on your arbutus breast—
Flinging its fullness of spray,
As the foam-flinging crest of your love
Sweeps up on my innermost shores,
And leaves me to compass the day
With a lustier glint in my eye,
A saltier thrill in my heart.

When I Hear Bells

When I hear bells resounding in my ears,
Like a bell buoy anchored off a perilous shore,
Whose hammers in mild weather lay the fears
Of thoughtful sailors, I can do no more
Than contemplate the planet and be glad
That seas are sometimes calm, dreading the hour
When undertowing groundswell lifts its mad
Upheaval with an avalanche of power
Too few of all the craft that voyage blind
Have strength to stand. Tonight as mad bells ring
Through tempests of my brain, I strive to find,
As rushing billows cockle up and cling,
If I have strength to hold the wheel and ease
The hooker of my mind through troughs like these.

The Unknown Soldier

"Out of the tomb I speak:
I have had praise enough to make
A movie hero's cheek
Blush to the hair roots, but I loathe it all—
I stifle in this unknown soldier's tomb.
I was a wastrel who despised the gloom
Of solemn dignity, went winging free

From town to town with other birds like me—
Seeing the sights, stage-johnnying the girls,
Getting all tangled up in tangled curls
Till there was nothing else to do but run
And try another town. An hour's fun,
Then heartache, broken vows, and one dull trip
Across the ocean on a cattle ship
Doling out grain. The critters mooed all night,
Driving me almost nutty with their fright.
But stuck in Liverpool with five weeks' pay
I found a pub and drank there twice a day
To work the fantods off and see the town.
The sour English slums soon got me down,
And I was back in Uncle Sam's domain
When war broke out. A military train
Rolled drums and banners through my crazy brain
Till I said, 'Well, here goes,' signed up to fight
Like many another harum-scarum wight;
Got sent across, went out and raised high hell,
And found myself next day A.W.O.L.
In Gay Paree where Yanks were treated fine
As long as dough held out. Then up the line
My regiment was ordered. Was I scared?
Such horrors reached us of the way men fared
In front-line trenches! (No one closed an eye
Except at noontime when the sun was high
And warm enough to let them catch a wink;
The clammy mud and vile inhuman stink
Of human bodies rotting, and the drag
Of midnight hours that would sag and sag
Till some put pork on strings and played with rats
To keep them from completely going bats)—
All this was told us by the grapevine route
Till we said, 'Why should any sane galoot
Come to this awful country overseas,
For days of horror, heartache, and disease,
And cannon roaring, booming overhead?'
The most of us would rather far be dead
Than live like this. My soldiering was brief—
I poked my fool head up to find relief,

And found it for a time. Then diggers came
Looking for some of us unknown to fame,
Shoveled me up and carried me back home
To mix me with my cheated country's loam
In this boneyard. My rest was at an end,
For solemn statesmen came. Have I no friend
Can save me from their chatter and their flowers,
Their insincerities, their pomps and powers?
The weight of them is heavy on my breast.

"O buddies, pacing here to guard my rest,
Have mercy on me, spirit me away
To some lone country graveyard where the spray
Of their incessant spouting cannot find
My tired ears. Let me sleep with my kind
As you will sleep when your brief watch is done,
And all retreats and reveilles are one.

"Fame is a heavy thing—that lot is best
That goes the common way of all the rest."

Sunlight on the Spray

Roll me the emerald comber bathed in sunlight
That rises with the rising of the sea,
Accompanied by wind whose breeziest flight
Waits full flood tide; each wave-swept rock a key
Tuned for the touch of its unerring hand;
And when each note is struck the sinewy sun
Dances with veils of spray on sparkling sand
In naked freshness where the long waves run.

Showers of silver bursting on my eyes,
Like northern lights above clean Arctic snow,
Kindle my fancy till I half surmise
I see on rocks and reefs where breakers blow
Voluptuous mermaids leaping from the bay
To sparkle in the sunlight on the spray.

To a Tree

I often wondered, tree, today I know
How you withstood the buffets of the years,
While all around your plot would come and go
The boles and branches of your short-lived peers.
In youth your fibres fought with mighty bowlders
And field rocks bluntly stationed to retard
The rearing of your trunk above the shoulders
Of this fair western slope. You struggled hard
And twined your roots about them, clinging fast
With vicelike grip. Your neighbors' roots branched free
Of congregating rocks. Then came the blast,
And your prime obstacles had proved to be
Protecting anchors that the stout line gale
Could not uproot. Triumphant veteran, hail!

East Wind

There is a lingering northeast wind that sends
Corroding chill into the atmosphere,
Driving unlighted waves to futile ends
On unresponsive rocks. Fog rolling near
Blots out the sun. My sloopboat barely crawls.
Off shore a tossing bell buoy, clanging, plies
Incessant warning; and the cold sea walls
Grow ominous when a bulging comber flies
Savagely toward my bow. I quickly throw
The anchor, strain each nerve, and listening, feel
Boats all about me in distress that know
How breakers close at hand may suddenly steal
Up on the fleet and crush us at one blow,
Dooming our fortunes to the undertow.

226

Of Spruces

The cheerfulness of sunlight and the calm
And satisfying restfulness of green
Conspire in groves of spruce to yield a balm
On sunny days that keeps my heart serene—
For I was born where spruces amble down
To check the glint of sunlight on the bay,
Blending the balsam in their coats of brown
With scent of driftwood, kelp, and caraway.
And when long beams at sunset filter through
The openings between the tall spruce trees,
And I see silhouetted one or two
Gaunt herons settled for the night's long peace,
Cloud banks in me are broken up to flare
Like afterglow in delicate evening air.

American Granite

These rocks hold water pockets that endure:
Drive through their seams a new artesian drill;
Or quarry old-time lewis holes and fill
Their lowest depths with dynamite in sure
And careful measure. Blast, and watch the pure
Streams gather up the sunshine like the rill
That flashed from Moses' rod when Israel
Stood famished, gazing down the aperture.

These rocks hold more than water; in their yield
Of color, contour, symmetry, and strength
Abides the flinty character that steeled
Our fathers for great deeds. Throughout the length
Of this dishevelled continent yet stand
Blocks to rebuild the temple of our land.

New Year

Sad is the farewell of another year
When youth has passed the tropics and must steer
Into the northern straits of chilling age
Where icebergs loom to mock and spur the rage
That rises in us as we contemplate
Their monumental beauty, and the fate
That winnowed all our early dreams to dust;
We only say farewell because we must.
Currents of wind and tide are setting strong
Into the Arctic where the nights are long
And cold and deep, where resolution fails
To rouse us for a trek on icy trails—
And all ambitions merge themselves in one:
To chart the unbuoyed course beyond the sun.

Leaves

Some leaves are plucked by whirlwind,
Some by frost;
And some high oak leaves cling
However tossed
By hurricane or numbed
By rain and chill—
Cling and hang on throughout
The seasons till
Spring dances round again.
Her gay allure
So little counts with those
That could endure
The perilous time, they strive
No more to stay,
And drop contented in
Untired clay.

PART IV

Tides

I

The salt that permeates the human frame
Tallies a like proportion to the brine
That purifies the sea; and as the tides
Of ocean wax and wane about the cliffs
And marshes of the globe, so rise and fall
Within the human sphere the tides that flood
And ebb with ever varying weal and woe,
Until the last ebb tide forgets to turn.

II

Our daily round itself is like the tide:
The same but not the same; one morning breaks
Like flood tide on a rocky shore—a lift
Of buoyant vigor teeming in the blood,
Teeming, mounting, tumbling into joy
Through muddy gaps and craggy crevices,
Releasing slumber from our sluggish brains
As waters lift the rockweed from the bowlders.
A fragrance rises in us like the tang
Of spindrift on the tips of crowding waves;
And breezes springing in the coves that lay
Deep wallowing in mud an hour before,
Urge us to greet the sun as herring gulls
Hail fishing boats careening up the bay.
On other days we rise to smell the mud
Cloying our nostrils—dilatory winds
Lapse to an oily and foreboding calm.
Sharp ledges rear their jagged points and show
A treacherous, broken shore line; tide-rip currents
Carry us on the reef despite all skill;
A storm wind rising drives the battering waves
To swamp our ventures till they break apart
Wrecked on goring ledges black and bare.

III

The variation of terrestrial tides
From scarce a fathom on the Arctic Circle
Or placid South Sea isles, to Fundy's Bay
Where flood tide rushes and goes tearing through
The rock-strewn narrows with a headlong plunge
Till sixty feet of cliff is drowned in sea,
Tallies the varying moods of human fate.

IV

The mechanistic chart of human tides
Is dotted with false soundings: flowing life,
Like flowing sea, is tentacled with new
And ever newer reaches of surprise.
No mean tide flows in man or in the deep:
From day to day in man, from tide to tide
In ocean, all that flies, or walks, or swims
Knows change, scarce felt, yet ever recurring change,
Forever foiling gray monotony,
Outwitting man's attempts to find the key,
The magic key to turn within a lock
It always fumbles for but never fits.
As late June tides rise higher every hour
Until the full moon brims the circling sea
To overflowing fullness, and the rocks
Untouched by ordinary tides succumb
Before the moving of the quiet waters,
And even the grasses on the bank are licked
By unaccustomed tongues of salt; and men
Who dwell along the coast are lifted up
Like Peter when he walked upon the water;
So flows the spirit of the lowliest life
Through channels of good fortune gliding in
Triumphant over hidden shoals and bars,
Halting on mossy plots of greenery;
And as in wintry hours the same droll moon
Heaps up December tides when blustering winds
Are loosened from northeastern corridors
Of ocean's madhouse and come fully armed

230

To wreck our proudest sloopboats on their moorings—
So tragedy comes stalking through the bays
And estuaries of the kingliest life
And will not be denied till winds go down
And ebb tide reassumes its quiet ooze.

The heart of life defies exactitude;
No measure yet devised can square the circle,
Or multiply diameters by rules
Precise enough to tell what circles are
Beyond dispute or cavil. Like the stone
The Roman soldiers placed at Jesus' tomb,
Shored up and buttressed—seal them strong as death,
There's always something rolls the stones away.
This evanescent something, like the tide,
Eludes the instruments, and gambols free,
Defiant, anarchistic—'tis the soul
Of every one of us: the kicking child
At eight months in his mother's weary womb
Struggling to be released; the two-year-old
Running away from home; the adolescent
In fellowship with danger, hurling fear
And caution overboard that man's blind course
Over the sea of darkness might be charted;
And most of all today it is the goad
Driving the scientist to find the key
That will unlock the doors and open up
The secret corridors of human fate:
A priest, he stands within his cubicle
Experimenting on the essences
That constitute the globe; and like the priests
Who sang their matins and their evensongs
In centuries gone by, this anchorite
Finds mystery grown more mysterious
A thousandfold as he divides the atom
And finds a universe in embryo
With proton like the sun, and whirling round
In microcosmic space electrons spinning;
And over all, before his very eyes,
Substance and matter ebbing quite away.

V

The flooding or receding universe
Of which men reason marks the tides that rise
And fall upon the restless shore of that
One universe of universes stored
With myriad hypotheses—the mind,
The inquiring mind of man that seeks to know
Where knowledge baffles, and where instruments
Are helpless to discern what lies beyond
The spiral nebulae or lies within
The speediest electrons that erode
The coast line of the atom, ever beating
Their midget waves on its elusive shores.
Man's mind it was that felt the tide go out
Leaving the flaming craters of the sun
To cool and harden as the ages ebbed,
Until at last the world, a frozen mass,
Should stagger on its circling path alone.

Man's mind it was that felt the tides return
With atoms being born in space to brim
This dark depressing ebb-tide sea once more:
Pollen of radiance blown between the stars
And flowering on our planet's atmosphere
Brightens the mind of man as bubbles cheer
A zealous five-year-old; and like the pipe
The five-year-old dips down in soapy water
That now brings forth a myriad-colored globe
Of pulsing light, and now brings nothing forth:
So man creates from his peculiar mind—
From ebbing, flowing tides within that mind—
Answers to human longing, then too soon,
The bubble bursting, blows and blows in vain.

VI

The law bequeathing man his cooling earth
Wrought on his mind a blight like that the fruit
Was fabled to have wrought on Eve, and all
The human race through her; and round that law
Clustered a star-cold galaxy of laws,

232

With mechanistic and material
Foundations at the very heart of life:
Faith shoved aside, free will destroyed; and all
The grandeur and nobility of man
Dragged out to ashes till he found himself
Naught but a speck upon a lowly planet—
A twofold biochemical machine,
An astronomic midget lost in space.
When Arnold saw the buoyant tide of faith
Turn and go out until he only heard
"Its melancholy long-withdrawing roar
Retreating to the breath
Of the night wind down the vast edges drear
And naked shingles of the world,"
He heard the note that crowned the century
With strophe and antistrophe of gloom,
Denying man one glimpse of noontide light,
Impounding in his breast a dry despair.

Then let us hail the flood tide that is rising
In quiet halls of questing scientists
To heap the unnavigable basin full;
And open doors that Science never proffers,
Into the spacious treasure house of truth;
Welcome new regions of the unknown shadow
That lengthens more with lengthening of the light;
Welcome again the blessed argosies
Of personality, free will, and wonder—
The hulls of expectation moving ever
Above the wallowing wrecks of space and time;
The indeterminate fleet at Nature's heart
Once more launched boldly by the very band
Whose heresies had chased them from the seas.
These anchorites within their cubicles
Have given us an earth and Heaven new,
And that drear Heaven and earth that plundered us
Of metaphysic hope has passed away,
And Haeckel's sea of darkness is no more;
A time to build the new Jerusalem
On this glad earth of singing birds and flowers

And mould it to our dreams is here at last;
A million million years before the sun
Slips over the edge to join the white-dwarf stars.
A million million years to blot out pain
And wipe away disease from humankind
When mourning, crying, grief shall be no more;
Leisure to navigate the stratosphere,
And cruise for pleasure in among the stars;
A million million years to launch new fleets
And voyage to a more congenial planet
Among the golden galaxies of Heaven.
The ear of man can then hear morning stars
Singing together in the early dawn,
For he himself will drift among the stars
As now he drifts about bay-cinctured islands—
Drift to the source of cosmic rays and hear
Ten thousand times ten thousand voices singing
Such hymns as angels of the upper air
On Holy Night between the wandering star
And quiet fields of Bethlehem proclaimed:
Peace and Good Will, Good Will and Peace to Men.

Notes on the Poems

Cooting. "Coot" is the word used in northern New England for the surf duck or scoter. The word was corrupted from "scoter" to "scooter," then shortened to "scoot," and finally to "coot." It has no connection whatever with the mud hen, which is the genuine American coot. There are four varieties of "coot" on the coast— the gray coot, the butterbill, the patchhead and the whitewing. The last two mentioned are in this poem.

"The Stallion" is the favorite gunning rock three miles off from the mainland at Spruce Head.

"Tollers" was the word we invariably used for decoys.

Cod-Fishing. "Slack-salted" fish were those that required the minimum amount of salt to keep off the flies and preserve the flesh. Those heavily salted lost a great deal of the fish flavor.

"Snood hooks" were those that did not have a hole or eye through which to bend the line, but instead an enlarged flattened end to keep the ganging, wrapped around the hook, from slipping off. To us the hole or eye hook was a device for landlubbers or summer "rusticators."

The "slack-tide hour" was the hour around high water or low water when the tide was not running. At these times one's line went straight down.

Thanksgiving Shoot. "Brant-goose" is a local word for brant. To us the word is more intensive or emphatic than the correct term.

Wood-Chopping. "From peak to scarf" is the phrase used to designate the distance from the point at one end of the log to the edge of the bark at the other. For good measure in a cord of wood that distance should be four feet. Skinflints measured from peak to peak.

"Budded" means to feed on buds. Partridge were compelled to feed on birch buds when snow covered the ground.

Winter Evenings. "Pot-heads": the funnel-shaped, netlike contrivance at either end of the lobster pot with a round hole in the middle through which the lobster has to crawl to reach the bait inside. The knitting of these was one of the major employments of our winter evenings.

Before the Wind. "Fog-mull." A long-drawn-out spell of foggy weather.

Storm Visitor. "Redd up." To tidy up or put in order. The word was common a generation ago, but now is scarcely ever heard.

Captain Rivers. "Congress shoes." Shoes without buttons or laces. They were held firmly to the foot by means of soft wide bands of elastic inserted on each side of the ankle.

Fred Rowley. "Lucifee." A corrupt but extremely common pronunciation of the word *loup-cervier*—the Canadian lynx.

The 100% American. Lord Charnwood once said that the American nation was founded by a group of men who did not believe in democracy for three million people who did not believe in any government at all.

Tides. The nineteenth century was a century dominated by science, and we who were born at the latter part of that century were so influenced by its findings that we read reverently what any well-known scientist had to say about the problem of Ultimate Reality. The change I have tried to describe in this poem may be sharply illustrated by contrasting a quotation from Haeckel's *The Riddle of the Universe*, written in 1900, with a quotation from Eddington's *Science and the Unseen World*, written in 1929. The Haeckel quotation reads:

The great abstract law of mechanical casuality, of which our cosmological law—the law of substance—is but another and a concrete expression, now rules the entire universe, as it does the mind of man.

The Eddington quotation written almost thirty years later reads:

We have learnt that the exploration of the external world by the methods of physical science leads not to a concrete reality but to a shadow world of symbols, beneath which those methods are unadapted for penetrating. Feeling that there must be more behind, we return to our starting point in human consciousness—the one centre where more might become known. There we find other stirrings, other revelations (true or false) than those conditioned by the world of symbols.

SONNETS TO STEVE AND OTHER POEMS

PART I

Enduring Things

Praise earth for things that stale not: the first whiff
Of campfire smoke in grove or on the shore;
Deep corrugated waves when breezes stiff
Are furrowing the ocean; a wide moor
Tinted with autumn coloring; tall white clouds
Patrolling mountain tops; a fragile moon
Sentineled by the evening star; huge crowds
Of morning-glories touched with dew—how soon
The list brims over! Sailor, fisherman,
Proud horseback rider, ski enthusiast, come
Add to the list of pleasures, for you can,
That keep the full potential of their sum
Throughout the years, but only yield their best
To those who know how Love exalts the rest.

He Learned to Live

He learned to live beside the shelving sea
On days when tides ran low and waves were still;
The rich brown cliffs that slanted gracefully
From spruce-clad top to kelp-fringed base would fill
His heart to overflowing as he rowed
His little skiff along their magnitudes
In the clear air of twilight that bestowed
The mingled fragrances of sea and woods.

Herons stood through the silence low tide brings
As if they worshipped in these natural naves;
The gulls, with Mary's color on their wings,
Wailed *Miserere* over woods and waves;
And through this hour sunset moods unfurled
The loneliness and beauty of the world.

To J. S.

You are the surf upon the outer ledges,
The spots of calm on agitated seas,
The rich brown kelps that show their ruffled edges
At dead low tide, and you the offshore breeze
That brings a cooling fragrance from the ocean,
Driving midsummer's melting heat away,
Bestowing on the yachts their graceful motion
As they go winging up the moonstone bay.
You are the sea gulls breaking trails of beauty
In every pocket of the coastal air,
You are the granite cliffs whose guardian duty
Is keeping storms' erosion from this fair
Spruce-clad dominion whose bird-choiring aisles
Make earth a region on which Heaven smiles.

Coast Offerings

These granite ledges have the power to give
New strength when all the world needs strengthening;
The raging winds and coastal tides they fling
Aside as though they were but fugitive
And transient visitors blown down to live
Like us above these towering cliffs each spring.
Rest, too, in fullest measure they can bring
When cries for rest have grown imperative.

I lay me down upon this granite bowlder
To breathe the kelpy air, and hear the sea
Shut out the noise of war—its blaze and smoulder,
And sink into the granite gradually.
From syenite veins new strength flows into mine;
And rest comes drifting in from the drowsy brine.

California Coast

The California coast for many a mile
Sings to the world an oratorio
Whose major strains through salty breezes blow
Strength and good cheer enough to wipe all vile
Contagion from the land. Here the grand style
In music's offering rings fortissimo;
Here flowers that fringe the rolling sand dunes glow
Deeper than inland blooms. Here single file
The urge to Freedom lives in militant waves
That break themselves upon the indifferent sand.
What music in the effort! How each braves
Impossibilities of sea and land
In thunder tones as up the gradual stair
It crashes on the keyboard of the air!

Torching Herring

The streak of lawlessness that spattered through
Our nation from the start showed up in us
With least restraint when we were torching herring.
The Maine state law, prohibiting the use
"Of any inflammable substance in liquid form"
While catching fish within her coastal waters,
Was a ruse designed, we thought, to make us buy
Our herring from the weirs at fancy prices,
So we rebelled, and caught our lobster bait
By sneaking into narrow coves and guts
With muffled oars at night on the dark of the moon.

To a youth of fifteen it was a double joy,
This all-night trip to far-off bights and inlets:
The joy of catching fish was elemental,
A prime delight for adolescent boys;
And then there was the joy that Eve had started,
Rebellion's joy against the stifling laws
Designed to put a leash on liberty,
And keep the hound of wildness in us kenneled.

News of a herring strike six miles away
Had drifted to us on the flood of rumor,
So with a Friendship sloop as mother ship,
And two big dories trailing in her wake,
We took advantage of the evening breeze
That sang along the ruffled evening sea,
And sailed away to keep our rendezvous.

Zeke Andrews, senior member of our crew,
Illiterate, revengeful, saturnine,
His whiskers black, his hair an iron gray,
Never without a chew of white wax gum
Between white teeth incredibly preserved,
Had passed his days with dories, traps, and buoys.
Manoeuvring in an orbit all his own,
Unwilling to let others lobster near him,
He lost Hog Island to his wife's own brother,
And all the wealth he had in a dragged-out lawsuit.
Whenever he spoke he spoke with emphasis,
Saying "By Jesus," slapping his big hand
Down flat on any surface he could reach,
Perhaps your knee if you were near enough,
Stomping his cowhide boot for reinforcement,
His deep gargantuan voice and heavy hand
Filling the farthest reaches of the galley.
He stayed away from church, and looked on preachers
As ladies' men who could not tie a bowline,
Or take a porpoise from a mackerel seine;
Hence he was numbered with the town's ungodly.
But he could tell about a vicious shark
Attacking him one morning at his nets,
Or of a giant turtle from the south
That tore his seine to shreds and got away,
Or of a whale that rose beside his boat
And showered him with rainbow-tinted spume,
And tell these tales with such fresh metaphors
We lived them over with him as he spoke.

His son, proud owner of the good sloop *Flash*
That took us on the trip, was twenty-one,

And full of laughter as the summer sea.
Just married, with a baby on the ways,
Full of odd pranks and wayward practical jokes,
Such as emptying cans of sweetened milk
Into my brother's brand-new fishing boots,
He walked the deck correcting everything:
A frayed rope here, a grommet there
Would catch his eye, out would come his knife,
And he would transform disarray to order.
The *Flash* was new, he loved her as his wife,
Perhaps a little more, at least she feared so.
He loved to sail whenever northwest squalls
Made sailing dangerous, for hairbreadth 'scapes
To him meant full-time living—he guffawed
When capsized sloops were mentioned by his dad.

The third grown member of this casual crew,
A blue-eyed Saxon of colonial stock,
Our upright father, who had spent his life
In uncongenial work on a Coast Guard station.
A sense of duty chained him to the task
Like Samson at the mill. His seven children
And dark-eyed Irish wife laid claims upon him
Eight months of every year. When summer came
He was another creature—building boats,
Playing with lobster pots and mackerel nets,
A boy again, the dew of youth still on him.
At fourteen he had sailed with Captain Sheerer
On a long voyage in Caribbean waters,
And he would tell us of his escapades
In colorful ports upon the Spanish Main,
Until we wished his Puritan heritage
Had rested on his heart a bit more lightly.
Shoulders he had to carry mighty loads,
A spirit strong to bear yet heavier burdens;
To us he seemed impervious to decay.

The other three were striplings in their teens,
Two of us brothers, and a neighbor lad,
Who came along to share in the excitement.

To all of us congenial work was play,
And this unorthodox demand of brawn
A challenge so appealing to our minds
That we were restless for the starting hour.

We had not long to wait. Darkness swooped down
A little after six. White cotton-batting rolls
Were tied with wire on long iron rods,
And saturated well with kerosene,
One lashed across the bow of either dory.
Two rowers, each with two long white-ash oars,
Sat on the thwarts and pulled, while in the bow
A third man stood, at ready, with the dip net.
A lighted match was dropped upon the torch
And out of the darkness flames shot up toward heaven.
We rowers pulled like slaves of ancient Rome
Who manned the galleys, but the only lash
We knew was our ambition to see the fish
Boil up and up beneath the rising flame
That shone around the bow of either dory.
The faster we rowed the faster swam the fish,
Leaping at times completely out of water.
It was impossible, Zeke said, to tell
Which was the more excited, boys or herring.
Great dip-nets-full were thrown about our feet,
Oozing the fruity odor of live herring;
Fish scales were glittering everywhere we looked;
Our cheeks were flaked with little disks of white
That drew our skin taut and assailed our eyelids.
Our feet were clamped so tightly in the load
We could not wrench them free to aid our rowing.
The dory getting lower in the water
Became more sluggish, harder to manoeuvre,
And soon her gunnels leveled with the tide.
We dared take in no more, rowed to the *Flash*
And emptied out our cargo on her deck.
Then back for more we started—but a signal,
Agreed upon beforehand, from a flashlight,
Told us that fish wardens were lurking near;
So down into the water went our torch

With a sizzling noise that dwindled into silence,
And we were left in darkness doubly dark
After the blaze we had been living in.
The alarm proved false; belated summer folk,
Drawn by the light, had gathered on the shore,
Urged by the flame of curiosity.
Fresh rolls of cotton batting were unloosed,
New cans of kerosene, and we were off
To dip another load. The work went on
Until we brimmed the *Flash's* deck with bait,
Two hundred bushels crowning our long night's labor.
At half-past three we started back toward home,
The grown-ups sailing, we dissolved in slumber,
Slumber that only drowsy boys can know.
We slept the subterranean sleep of youth,
Dead to the salmon-colored sun that rose
Out of the eastern sea. Back to the mooring,
The dipping out, filling barrels, salting,
Took five heartbreaking hours. Soft feather beds
Invited us to sleep—the only urge
Our weary bodies knew. We wanted more,
Already drunk with sleep, we wanted more.

Tomorrow we would tempt the green crustaceans
With fresh new bait, but nothing more today
Save sleep, more sleep, nerve-mending hours of sleep.
Tomorrow we would hope for better fishing,
Hope, steadiest star in the fisherman's galaxy,
The North Star of his circumnavigation,
And like that star too dim at times to steer by,
Hidden too many nights, too many dawns,
Too many nights and dawns of cloudy weather,
But ever the torch that lures him on and on.

November Interlude

Pay heed to soft November days
When brown leaves snuggle on the ground,
And valleys teem with amber haze
That blurs the sharpness on the round
Unmoving canopies of oaks;
When roosters crow as if they knew
Some lusty secret that would coax
Hard winter to be kind to you.

The twittering chickadees declare
An Indian spring; the blue jays call
In major tones that rob the air
Of autumn chill; and topping all
The chorus of a thousand crows
Invades the valley till the dread
Of nipping blasts and drifting snows
That numb the countryside has fled.

And if perchance the niggard sun
Peers out upon these late fall days,
The raindrops on the alders run
To greet him with white pearls of praise;
The birds grow still and preen their wings,
The colors on the dead leaves play,
The mist along the valley flings
Its gray robe off and streaks away.

Girl Seen in an Art Gallery

Her soul, the spirit of the evening star
When balmy April airs invest the earth
With gentleness too delicate to mar
The sea foam playing round the headland's girth;
The atmosphere that quivered on her lips,
A crescent moon's above a saffron sea
Where lacelike rigging of majestic ships
Reflects along the waters tremblingly.

246

She knew what dwelt in Fra Angelico's
Serene and happy soul at eventide;
She knew cathedral window tints of rose
In old French towns where she would gladly hide;
She felt herself too far from home, and sought
Foundations our New World provided not.

Deceitful Calm

How can one who has seen this shore in storm
Believe what here spreads out before his eyes?
Low water round uncovered ledges lies
In stillness so subdued and uniform
That one might think neap tides would never swarm
Into the cove again. Only the cries
Of gulls and hawks that strut and gormandize
On crabs and mussels keep conviction warm
That Time has not stood still. And yet beneath
The heavenly sunrise calm of this clean bay
Repulsive sharks are tearing dragons' teeth
Through helpless schools of mackerel; dogfish prey
On cod and haddock; and some tidal wave
Waits to trap man in an unsuspected grave.

A Fiancée's Night Thoughts

"For three intolerable weeks
Depressing moods have crept around
My heart, as some night prowler sneaks
Into a room with scarce a sound
Where sleepers stir—their loud hearts pound,
They feel a fear they cannot see,
Breathless, choked, and terror-bound,
They writhe in restless agony.

At two o'clock the stillness wakes
Me up; I lie and toss and think
Forbidden things till the white-throat breaks
The spell; I tremble on the brink
That separates the mind's mad link
From elemental sanities;
Great gargoyle eyes before me blink
To shatter all my vanities.

'Is there,' my sleepless head inquires,
'Enough of light within his face
To kindle satisfying fires,
And make his soul a warming place
For hosts of friends? Or shall I grace
A helpmate faithful, stupid, good,
Who never once will try to trace
Blue shadows in the magic wood?

'And when he tries to understand
Imaginings that float and break
Like bubbles in my mind, his hand
And tongue-tied heart will grope and ache;
And knowing not what path to take
Will give up, calling women fine
But glittering bubbles. Will that wake
My pity enough to make him mine?' "

After a Storm

After a storm brown ledges glow
Like northern stars on Arctic snow;
The waves pound in with fuller thump
Although the calm has smoothed each lump
On the grape-green surface, leaving beneath
Strong undertow with shattering teeth.
The trees in moss more pensive stand,
As if they wondered what gaunt hand
Had thrust itself through last night's air,

Uprooting their brothers, and seeking to tear
From their own firm trunks each parrying limb,
Now clean as an athlete's after a swim.
The clouds are gone that trailed buff wings
Down close to the boughs where the damp still clings
And the goblet of sky holds many a white
Ebullient cloud shot through with light.
The chickadees gather in groves of fir
To carol their joy that the rage and stir
Of the night before have given place
To the turquoise sky and mirrored face
Of cove and harbor where tossed-up shells,
Brown kelp, and eelgrass' lusty smells
Conspire to make complete amends
In a moving peace as the great storm ends.

Vacation Mood

Away with efficiency! Man was made
To putter around in the garden shade,
Think a few thoughts, dream many dreams,
Sample, experiment, sever what seems
From things as they are; gaze at night sky,
At the sea and the mountains, cast a fly
In a boyhood brook, sprawl in the sun,
Or in the woods' shadow—walk or run
As the spirit wills. Life might be good
Were it not for our plunging, acquisitive mood.
Thoreau defied it. Why cannot we
Cast off the burden of doing—and *be*?

Bequest to my Sons

To you I will the lean-yeared heritage
My fathers willed to me—granitic land
Fringing a coast whose northern winters stand

Defying all attempts to soothe their rage;
To you I will my own lean equipage,
Scorned as a horse-and-buggy dowry—banned
In our swift day—yet ready at command
To teach the patience of a friendlier age.

I will you hope to face the perilous day
On which the world has fallen: crude machines,
Unreckoned with, smite people hard and gray
As bowlders in New England's parched ravines;
Tame them, and taming, win the strength to slay
New dragons coming on to blight new scenes.

Vacation End

Far off the sea gulls wheel and cry,
And near at hand the glossy crows
Swoop down on me till I can hear
The creaking hinges of their wings;
A chipmunk leaps from bough to bough,
And partridges with cautious tread
Are visible, as one is now,
Showing his shapely gray-brown head,
And mingling with the underbrush
Till I can scarcely mark the line
Where boughs begin and feathers end.
His drumming violates the hush,
And brings me up where I can see
The glistening harbor's sparkling flash
Shine through the spruces here and there
Like diamonds in a woman's hair.

When twilight turns the upper boughs
From green to gold, a deeper hush
Subdues the woods, the manifold
Bird noises cease; only the rush
Of waves along the shore keeps up
Its endless music; now and then

A quawk upbraids the pewter sky
For the discomfort of her nest;
These, and the night wind's chilly sigh
Among the branches half-protest
Against too great a sense of calm
And loneliness. Then I arise
And, like the quawk, add groans and sighs,
But mine are of wide streets whose din
I soon shall be a captive in.
Would this do for a summer creed?
"Man has one elemental need,
One only; all the others pass
Like butterflies through summer grass:
To strike deep roots in earth and know
The peace wild nature can bestow."

The Western Meadow Lark

The Western meadow lark in spring,
Secretive bird, can make one whole
Beyond all other birds that fling
Their joy toward heaven's white-flowered bowl.

He greets the umber light of dawn
With notes as pure as those that broke
On Wasatch heights before the fawn
Fell under fear's restraining yoke.

He calls his mate with bubbling love
Made vibrant in a reedlike throat;
The cooing murmurs of a dove
Are harsh beside his mellow note.

The midday glare subdues his song,
But hoarding up his strength he breaks
The evening silence clear and long
As sunset gilds the Utah lakes.

The flowing joy he brings to me
Sweeps through my doors of hope until
I feel the world he sings to me
Lies just beyond death's window sill.

Return to New England

I love the old New England ways,
The vanishing New England speech,
The salt that saturates the haze
On every bleak New England beach.
I love the gentle snow that falls
On soft green fir and birch tree white,
That decks with pearl the gray stone walls,
And calms the coming on of night.

Around the head of Tremont Street
I gaze on faces whose imprint
Three centuries needed to complete
Three centuries of New England flint;
Ancestral fires burn in their eyes,
And signal messages to mine.
Who says our land declines and dies?
It ripens like Egyptian wine.

I board a dim North Station train,
And from the diner look to see
Old landmarks on the way to Maine
The years have made so dear to me.
Watching the big flakes saunter down
On farmhouse, pasture, thicket, glade,
I feel my brow relax its frown,
And hear my heart sing undismayed.

I reach the house where I was born,
And gaze there while the falling snow,
Circling, covers all things worn
With wreaths like those my thoughts bestow
About the place. My heart is full,

Full of this region that is home—
These woods, this cove, these cliffs whose pull
Holds like great anchors through mad foam.

Aunt Delia and the Alabama Claims

Among the black sheep of the neighborhood
Was one whose blackness added streaks of jet
To our ungainly flock. She drank from brooks
That none of us had sampled, glittering rills
Of ancestry, whose subterranean streams
Trickled through the pastures of her spirit
When all our streams were dry. The alchemy
Transmuting these rills to the world's great waters
Came from a fleet of ships, her father's pride,
That ventured out to every port on earth,
Carrying from the Orient great loads
Of silk and tea and spices that enriched
The family heritage, and something more,
To our small seaport town more potent still,
A gloss of bright gentility that reached
To this rejected member of the flock.

The gold and spices mattered not to her;
Blue-eyed, petite, and willful, she forsook
Her home at seventeen for a romance
With an illiterate fancier of horses
Who worked a summer in her father's stable.
One evening when the town clock's minute hand
Took centuries to move from nine to ten,
He coaxed her to climb down from the bedroom window.
Although her deed was ample evidence
That the plunging fiery spirit of her fathers
Was still alive, convention's acid chill
Tempered the hazard of a further plunge
As brine-charged water tempers iron drills
Brought red-hot from the anvil; hence her fling
Labeled her as a piece of doubtful metal,

And she was tossed out to the rubbish pile
As worthless scrap behind the family forge.

And so she came to live as one of us
In a little rocky village by the sea,
A place of stone sheds, fishing boats, and wharfs,
And cottages that cluttered up the shore,
Distinguished only by its poverty
(Unless, of course, one reckons cliffs and spruces,
And long white combers capering in at twilight);
Her husband, one more teamster hauling stone,
Herself, at times a daughter of the rich,
Proud of her name, lording it over us
With her superior ancestral airs;
At other times a sister of the lowly,
Scorning the shipyard king who cast her out,
Employing short, derogatory words
To stigmatize his ruthless search for wealth,
And ridicule his futile family pride.

Then all at once a shower of gold came down
From Heaven, or Hell, to Delia and her spouse.
The *Alabama* claims that dragged along
For years and years through court and super court
At length were settled, and the treasure chest
Of her paternal ship king was replenished
With gold for all his many bottoms sunk
By Raphael Semmes and a piratic crew
Of English tars impressed as Southerners
Who cruised from Africa to Newfoundland
In the *Alabama*, fastest ship afloat,
Destroying, burning, sinking, capturing,
For the Stars and Bars, huge barks and brigantines,
Tall full-rigged ships and graceful clipper craft,
And Bedford whalers loaded deep with sperm
Whose flames delighted Semmes as they arose
Like golden chains uniting earth and heaven—
A glorious sight amid the dregs of war.

"England will never pay," her father said,
Whenever the *Alabama* claims arose,

And showed he meant it by the careless way
He left all mention of it from his will.
His cast-off daughter reaped her share of gold—
A meagre share it was, but to her mind,
Untutored and erratic, it surpassed
The fabled glory of Potosi's mines.

"Aunt Delia's rich! Aunt Delia's rich!" was cried
From door to door, waking to life the town.
A fairy tale come true before our eyes
Tinted the glow that hung above the elms,
And softened outlines of obtuse stone walls.
Into that glow we went and thought of ways
That riches might announce to us their coming:
We thought of ambergris that might drift in,
And gold of Captain Kidd lodged under bowlders
Along the shore, or on some lonely island
Beneath a scraggly spruce three-quarters dead.
The leaden drabness of our poverty
Set off still more the unexpected gold
That fell on Delia and her family.
The American dream was hers in sunlit force,
And we stood basking in its afterglow.

"What will she do with all this wealth?" we asked,
Nor did we have to wait long for an answer.
Soon a new dwelling rose on the edge of town,
And back of it a much-remarked-on cookhouse—
For Delia, grown fastidious, found herself
Unable to endure the scent of cooking.
Into her new-built barn there pranced a pair
Of stone-gray horses, and a glossy surrey,
Then two lace nets, with fringes and red tassels,
Trappings for gentry's horses in warm weather.

Lovers of horseflesh hung around the barn
On Sundays to discuss with Mel, her husband,
The fine points of this pair of thoroughbreds,
Nervously chomping, whinnying in their stalls.
Aunt Delia's husband had a month of Sundays
To idle round the stable, for with wealth

He threw aside his job, resolved to find
The promised glories of a life of ease.
Plain ignorance, however, handicapped
The expanding freedom of his idle hours.
He drove his new team to the city mornings,
And drove it back into the barn at night;
Secured a new gold watch, and then another,
Although he could not tell the time of day;
And when, maliciously, folks asked the time
He held both watches up before their eyes.
He bought a pair of long black driving gloves,
And let the tailor fashion him one suit
To match Aunt Delia's ocean of apparel,
New hats, new dresses, new lace veils, and all
The various shoes the tradesmen of the city
Could wheedle her to buy. They took her hand
As she alighted smartly from her carriage,
And flattered her as she had not been flattered
Since her father claimed her auburn curls at four
The sweetest shower of gold that ever fell
To any home on earth or on the sea.

Nor did she lack for flatterers at home:
Her list of friends expanded overnight,
Fair-weather friends who listened to her story,
And praised her luck, and praised her brood of children.
Neighbors dropping in would stay for dinner
And bring home stories of her youngsters playing
Marbles with golden coins, and losing them
In the tall grass, or in between the ledges
That jutted from the earth about her yard.
Once when a neighbor called there in the morning
Aunt Delia said, "Guess what I did today?"
Then added, never waiting for an answer,
"I let my Mellie have three hundred dollars!"
"What did you do that for?" the neighbor asked.
"To see what the damned fool would do with it," she chuckled.
Her horse-enamoured spouse knew what to do.
Long had he cast an eye on Ames's filly,
White-stockinged Belle, the smartest colt in town.
A hundred dollars was our topmost price

For thoroughbreds, so when Mel offered three,
Cautioning, "You'd better think it over,"
His neighbor hesitated, gravely torn
Between the gold of this fantastic offer,
And eagerness to keep her as his own.
Not quite could he resist the tempting coin,
Then cursed himself for his weak-willed decision.

After one year of this extravagance
Their youngest child fell suddenly ill and died.
"God's punishment for all their foolish spending,"
Some neighbors said, and others merely wondered.
The stricken mother vowed to have a funeral
The likes of which the town had never seen.
She bought a casket lined with silk and satin,
With handles washed in gold, and ordered flowers
That jammed the house with too much scent and color;
Black horses came with shiny harnesses,
Attendants with white gloves and black Prince Alberts,
Walking beside the hearse as hired mourners,
Solemnly walking to the cemetery.
The neighbors stood awe-stricken at the sight,
Sorrow contending with astonishment.
'Twas whispered that a thousand dollars went
Into the making of this spectacle;
And if six thousand were her share of claims,
Aunt Delia's fall could not be long a-coming.

She went with checkbook to the city bank
A few months later, when the lean director
Came from behind his cage and said, "I'm sorry,
But all your balance seems to be expended."
She brought out piles of checkbooks still unused,
And asked if there had not been some mistake,
Repeating until endless repetition
Betrayed how shocked and numbed the news had left her.

Her importuning friends dispersed like swallows
That scurry southward at the first fall blast.
Her creditors came down like vultures on her,
Their smiles replaced by frowns and insolence.

The village neighbors kept on just the same,
Through ill as through good fortune uncondemning,
More sympathetic now that she was back
One of the poor with them. The pair of grays
Was swapped for two work horses Mel could keep
As necessary for a teamster's living.
Loved Belle was taken by a creditor
Who did not want her, but found little else
Around the place that he could turn to gold.
A little more than one year set aside
To play the Lady Bountiful resolved
Itself to memories in Aunt Delia's mind—
Sweetest among them presents she had given
To almost every workingman in town.
Robustious and energetic Mel
Declared himself far happier than before,
Viewing no more with hatred, scorn, or envy,
The long, dull hours of a man of ease,
Saying, "It's better to wear out than to rust out,"
As if he were the first on earth to say it.

The house went long unpainted, and the cookhouse
Was broken up for firewood in winter.
The children went away to other towns
And married like the rest of us. The village
Amused itself on winter nights with tales
Of Delia's brief excursion into wealth,
Unmatched before or since, feeling itself
A party to the legend that has given
Our seaport town a dubious distinction,
And brought warm smiles to many and many a neighbor
Who counts the episode a legacy
Worth more than all the *Alabama* claims.

Relaxing Hour

Do you remember a morning,
A fragrance-of-pineapple morning

After an earth-shaking storm?
Subdued, we sat on the beach
Conversing in quiet voices
About the night before.
Undertow was at work
Filling the furrows with granules
Of yellow-green light-catching sand
As it churned up the rockweed and eelgrass,
And glossy brown aprons of kelp.
The heightened peace that followed
The raging might of the gale
Had settled over the island,
And over the tops of the waves.
Even the gulls were subdued
In their clamor among the gray ledges;
And one, on a red spar buoy,
Looked long and long out to sea,
As if wondering how the same planet
That rode out the storm of the night,
Like a ship through a turbulent ocean,
Could sprinkle such halcyon peace
Over islands and harbor again.

By a Northern Sea

The moisture in the salt sea air
Tints petals deeper in these woods
Than Nature is inclined to spare
To lofty mountain solitudes.

Here mussel shells beneath tall trees,
Dark blue inlaid with pearl, reveal
To what green-laden rookeries
The crows and fish hawks nightly steal.

Spruce limbs that withered in the grip
Of northeast gales put on gray lace
To match the colors of a ship
Whose bones are withering near this place.

Great mounds of clam shells up the reach
Tell where the Indian tribes of old
Held festivals along the beach,
And silhouetted evening's gold.

Now motorboats disturb the bay
With racking sounds that never cease
To shout the passing of the day
Of birch canoes and primal peace.

The trees remain, the sea gulls call,
Bright ledges wait the rolling tides;
Machines encroaching may appall,
But cannot ruin what abides.

Evening Duet

Father and son sit quietly apart
And contemplate the stillness of the trees:
A lofty grove of spruce, its inner heart
Holds concentrated solitude. No breeze
Now stirs enough to move a single bough,
Mosses beneath the trees enhance the calm;
The father feels the need of quiet now,
Quiet that soothes the agèd like a psalm.

But to the boy's more pioneering mind
The spruces stand and strain to reach the sun,
Shoving the neighboring trees aside to find
The light they need for growth, and space to run.
One dreams of peace that he can anchor to;
The other hails dark woods to struggle through.

Nile Valley

The fertile valley of the Nile that rocked
The cradle of mankind, and bred the race

That built the Giza Pyramids, and shocked
The savage into courtesy—this place
Of camel caravans and ibis birds,
Of horses, water buffalo, and mules,
Of white felucca sails, mud huts, and herds
Of Pharaoh cattle, prehistoric tools—

This fertile valley tamed the restless tribes,
And taught them to renounce their wandering ways,
Subdued the desert beasts, and warned the scribes
That life goes on forever; through the haze
Of sandstorms, famine, locust blights, and flies,
This valley looked on Death and called it lies.

The Sea

Gaze out upon the earth-encircling sea,
Gaze long and long until you know for sure
That she has sealed you to her mystery,
That she has brined your spirit to endure.

Explore the beauty in her blue-green eyes,
That stirs imagination's boldest flight,
Wherein big rolling clouds by day arise,
And brilliant stars smile gaily through the night.

Observe a stillness in her calm sweet face
That makes our restless faces blush with shame,
A fundamental stillness flashing grace
Like graceful gulls that herald her acclaim.

Or watch that face when mighty tempests roar,
And note beneath its agitated thrills
A music that goes singing to the shore,
A grandeur more expansive than the hills.

Inhale the perfume of her foaming hair,
The odor of ripe fruits and fragrant flowers

That tinctures all the cool surrounding air,
And flutters wildly through the windy hours.

Heed well the inspiration of her voice,
Supreme among the agencies of earth
To thunder harmonies that should rejoice
The God that gave the stars and planets birth.

O sacred spirit of the sacred sea,
Open your gates and touch earth-weary men
With your magnetic wand, lift their ennui,
And give our fear-struck race new life again!

Bayberry, Rocks, and Spruces

Bayberry, rocks, and spruces
Staring endlessly
At the moving vastness
Of surrounding sea,
What magic in you quickens
A quiet joy in me?

Bayberry, rocks, and spruces
Yearning toward the sky,
Are there hidden voices
You have caught from high
Uncharted realms beyond the reach
Of mortal ear and eye?

Bayberry, rocks, and spruces
Hoarding up the sun,
How can you glow as if the world
Had only just begun
A midsummer of perfect bloom
That never would be done?

A Hummingbird

Green head and gossamer wings
Darting from nowhere suddenly,
Wings like cobwebs on morning-glory vines
At the dayspring's delicate hour,
Your gray-gold flashes in sunlight,
As you pause by an alder limb,
Hum, "Alders, be proud of your color!"
Gyrating creature of air,
Scarcely material essence,
Are you the midsummer madness
Born of looking at flowers?
Vision or bird, or both,
Your motion is your song—
A song so thrilling the yard
Upon your instant arrival
That the air can almost sustain you
Without the vibration of wings.

Sailor Philosophy

Life is a coil of rope:
Let it lie on the shore
In the sun of too much idleness,
It twists so full of kinks
That no one can straighten it out;
Mildew and rot creep in,
And grass shoots up through its decay.

But if we stretch it out
On boats and hauling lines,
Giving it little rest,
It frays and unravels,
And when our need is greatest,
Breaks in a northeast gale,
Tearing our boats from their moorings,
Strewing them over the sea.

Is there never a way to use wisely
This Gordian-knotted rope-coil of life?

Invocation

Waters of anguish rolling on my heart
In dark unceasing waves of cruelty,
From out that infinite expanse of sea
In my subconscious, measureless to chart—
Pound on and on and on, nor quite depart
Until this stony soul of mine is free
From all the incrustation and debris
That keep its tone beneath the tone of art.

And, most of all, take from its rocky shore
The barnacles of bitterness that grow
To lacerate kind hands that would restore
Poor shipwrecked souls; restrain your undertow,
And when the winds of passion cease to roar
Grant me the peace of evening's afterglow.

New England River Chill

In the long Connecticut Valley
How can love drink its fill
When spring repels each sally
With its clammy river chill?

It creeps into every mossy
Youth-inviting hollow
When the dogwood smile is saucy,
And swallow chases swallow.

It sinks to the very marrow,
It settles in the bone,
Cold as the frost on the harrow,
Or husbands sleeping alone.

264

It creeps from the river basin
To every swale and knoll;
This wave of chill on field and hill
Has pinched New England's soul.

Saint Joseph

"The Eastern Kings have little use for me,
The shepherds watch the baby with delight,
Stricken with years, I know not where to flee,
The angel's visit but a dream at night.
Young Mary is a welling spring of love,
The baby is as radiant as the Star;
But my place in this busy barn's alcove—
Oh, what am I—more than the swallows are?"

Joseph divined and well defined
Man's place in our hemisphere:
A bridegroom mouse behind his spouse,
From year to weary year
A shadowy haze in the dazzling blaze
Of wife and children dear.
His living heir, the American male,
Across the years cries, "Joseph, hail!"

A Frightened Girl's Lament
(First World War)

"Wind in the elms, why wail?
Bearer of sighing and moan,
Will I never, O never again hear the gale
Of laughter hid deep in your tone?

Wind of the night, move on,
Your tidings from Europe declare
Reunion with him a hope that is gone,
And life's final chapter, Despair.

Breezes at midnight, be still,
My heart can no longer abide
Your moaning and wailing man's passion to kill
As around old cathedrals you cried.

Wind of the dawn, spring up,
Dispel all these terrors of night;
Wrap earth in warm zephyrs, remove this dark cup;
Come quickly, and bring morning light!"

The Real Pied Piper

"What wouldn't we give to rid this town of rats!"
The burghers sighed, as they resumed their chairs,
Persuaded things had gone too far for cats
Or powdery poisons; each one sits and stares,

Hoping for some solution that might carry
Relief to Hamelin and its countryside,
Alive with filthy rodents come to harry
The crowded city like an earthquake's tide—

When all at once in steps a grisly stranger,
Girded with iron mail from head to toe,
And fingering a fife that hints of danger,
Who bluntly said, "I'll make the vermin go,

Only I'll have my price." "Take anything,"
The burghers cry, "take all we have and hold;
Rid us of this dread pestilence, then bring
Your full demands; we'll shower you with gold."

The guest without another word saluted,
And strode into the bustling market place,
Lifted his fife up to his lips and tooted
Strains of an irresistible martial grace.

266

The boys and young men listened to his playing,
Crowded the public square from farm and shed,
Till the whole town was tense with youth arraying
Themselves to tackle anything he said.

His speech was brief, "I call on you to shoulder
Weapons to rid this place of rats. Prepare
To follow me till cellar, street, and bowlder
Hide them no more. The foe is everywhere."

They formed their troops in squadrons and brigades,
Deployed their ranks on mountain, field, and hill,
Cleaned out the foe from alleys, streets, and glades;
Then suddenly the countryside went still.

The rats were gone, but youth had left the city,
Youth was the hostage drawn from Hamelin town;
No one who walked there could escape the pity
In old men's hearts and women's heads bowed down.

A corporal's guard was left—the feeble few
Unfit for service with the brave and fair,
Contrasting sadly with the radiant crew
That now lay folded in the mountain's care.

Gone was the girlish laughter, fresh as flowers,
And gone the lusty shouts of strapping boys,
Silent the playgrounds, full of weeds the bowers
Where lovers in the moonlight found new joys.

The rats were gone, but oh, the price exacted,
The price in loneliness, heartache, and tears;
The empty homes and empty tombs refracted
A devastating light through empty years.

On A Portrait of Mark Hopkins in the Faculty Room of Williams College

Intensity, I never knew your name
Until I saw Mark Hopkins' serious face
Look down with as devoted eyes of grace
As ever burned within a prophet's frame.
The strength the dark blue Berkshire Hills proclaim
Was his lean heritage, and helps us place
His passion for the uplift of the race
On the old New England stock from which he came.

Great teacher, as we contemplate your zeal,
Your daily walk with God, your search for truth,
Your sacrificial life and wide appeal
For Christian manhood in your country's youth,
We glimpse the log that many a student found,
Like Moses' bush, a spot of holy ground.

Early Marriage Song

Your hair is a sun-caressed garden
Through which I leisurely stroll
Breathing the musk of roses.

Your eyes are quiet coves
Into whose waters white birch limbs
Cast dappled reflections.

The curve of your neck
Is a delicate new moon
Over sycamore trees
In early April twilight.

Your warm pink cheeks
Are tea-rose petals,
Curls linger above them
Like honey-laden bees.

The breath of your nostrils
When fragrant with passion
Is a New England hillside
Fragrant with trailing arbutus
At the first melting onrush of spring.

The soles of your feet
Are water-lily pads
Stirred by evening breezes.

Your breasts are ripe pomegranates
Shining through green leaves at dawn
In the Virgin River valley of Utah.

When you stand at the mirror
Disrobing at night,
You are Arethusa,
And the green shimmering robe
Your rippling fountain.

Two dreams that were with me in youth
Took shape at my first glimpse of you:

The first, sunny hours of love
On a long sloping hillside in June,
Green and gray moss underneath,
Evergreen branches above,
And a startling prevision of you.

Then a world out of ugliness moved
Into Danaän beauty—men free
As they dream everywhere to be free—
A world in which Love holds the reins

And rides over Death and Despair;
Such a world I prophetically saw,
Still see emanating from you.

PART II

I

Knowing and living with and loving Steve
For fifteen sunlit years was wealth to prize;
I count his virtues, even as I grieve,
Virtues as steady as his dark brown eyes—
A gaiety of spirit unsurpassed,
A sense of humor that was all his own,
A thoughtfulness of others to the last,
When lacerating pains forced him to moan.
The moans he stifled or in part denied
Were kept from us as favors from a heart
That would allay our worry, not from pride,
But from desire to shoulder his own smart,
And key affliction to a Spartan strain,
While the sly fox was gnawing at his brain.

II

Earth does not want her fairest to survive;
Deep in her heart there are malignant fires
That break through outer crust and come alive
In spots once famed for sacrificial pyres;
And those old Aztec priests above the burning
Who sacrificed the dearest of a tribe
To appease the savage world's insatiate yearning
Accepted her demands and paid the bribe.
And we today who throw our stalwart sons
Into the crater of a global war,
Sparing our lame, and sly, and useless ones,
Merely yield earth what she is clamoring for.
Earth plucks her roses soon, but lets her weeds
Bloom on and on and multiply their seeds.

III

Why should a cell go wrong within the brain
Of such an innocent and lovely lad?
Aspiring, thoughtful, why must early pain
And death be his inheritance? What sad
Perversion of the world threw justice off

270

And doomed him from his birth? Is there a pry
Can tear these walls apart? Or must we scoff
At earth's fair promises that passed him by?
One writes, "When you go in among the flowers
Of your rose garden for a bright bouquet,
You always pick the bud or bloom that towers
Above the rest. And so with God." He may,
Perhaps, be right. But why did God allot
A child to suffer as a rose cannot?

IV

How could I say of flowers, "Please omit,"
Where Stephen was concerned? He loved them all.
First rose in bloom! His eyes devoured it:
He found the last blue gentian in the fall.
He gazed on morning-glory bloom in May,
And little did I think my favorite flower
Would be the symbol of his earthly stay,
His span contracted to a morning hour.
The morning-glory's secret—does it lie
In dews of evanescence? Would its grace
Be lost if it endured the brazen sky
Of garish noon? And would that sensitive face,
That morning-glory face have found life's sun
In its decline a disappointing one?

V

Within this shyest nature there was strength
Tough as the fibres of an ancient elm,
Where layer on layer, imbedded, weaves its length
In convolved twistings. He could overwhelm
Temptations his companions yielded to,
Endure privation like a Roman stoic,
Suffer great pain in silence, carry through
Hard tasks without one hint of the heroic.
He climbed the topmost branch of the tallest tree
To match his bigger brothers, never flinched
In swordplay, football, roughhouse—he would be
The last to say "Give up" when mauled and pinched.
And when the surgeon beckoned he was ready,
No morphia was required to keep him steady.

VI

We came upon Grand Canyon's southern rim
Just as the sun was blazoning designs
Of color rich enough to render dim
All other sunsets of all other shrines;
And he to whom fine scenery was boring,
A theme of satire for his back-seat crew,
Walked to the edge with me and stood adoring
The purple haze upon that vast purview.
He looked into my eyes and took my hand
And said, "Oh, Daddy!"—but could not express
In words the wonder which that Western land
Had quickened in his soul—sheer happiness
Lit up his face as sunset lit the haze;
His dark eyes mirrored what he could not phrase.

VII

I close the back door, stroll about the yard
And watch five clumsy puppies eat and play;
The adorable clumsiness of the Saint Bernard
Arrests me till I think of Steve and say,
"How he would love to watch these darlings roll,
Climb on each other, bite at each other's tails,
Lap milk from one another's faces, bowl
Each other over," and my courage fails
Thinking of him, lover of cats and dogs,
Chickens and cows, and all things round the place,
Now in the deep dark grave—bewildering fogs
Enshroud me in a world that could erase
This love of life embodied in a boy
Whose very presence was a quiet joy.

VIII

If there were comfort in communal grief
This were the hour to mourn—so many sons
Being blotted out might offer us relief
Knowing our boy among the shining ones;
Burning in tanks, colliding in the sky,
Torpedoed on a cold green northern wave;
Picked off in South Sea jungles, left to die

On coral reefs with no trace of a grave.
But Grief makes her abode in solitude,
In individual solitude alone—
A wasteland where all forests have been hewed,
And all moraines washed clean as rain-washed bone;
So inward is her gaze if trees there were
She scarce could tell a cypress from a fir.

IX

On summer afternoons he loved to sail
Among the many islands of the coast;
Learning each island's name and many a tale
Of shipwreck, buried treasure, pirate's ghost.
He learned the use of reef point, cleat and grommet,
The way to furl a mainsail, tie a knot,
And laughed aloud while skimming over the summit
Of bulging billows with the mainsail taut.
How can I hoist my sail and leave the mooring
Without his sweet companionship and cheer?
How can I love the sea and the wind roaring
As when he stood in the cockpit with me here?
How can I voyage on without my mate,
And shape my course through earth's now narrowing strait?

X

Here was the world he loved—this rim of tide,
And spruce-clad islands of Penobscot Bay,
Circled by lobster buoys the medricks ride,
Here he was happy as a thrush in May.
The little skiff he rowed since he was six,
The catboat he and I together sailed,
The codfish reel initialed, and the sticks
That served as swords when piracy prevailed—
These bear his superscription—not an oar,
Or rope, or path, or wide-limbed branching tree
That does not link him to this rocky shore,
At least as long as we have memory.
Each granite cliff he scaled recalls his name
Clear as if wrought in bronze and fringed with flame.

XI

What eagerness for life shines in that face,
That boyish face, with wisdom like a man's;
The lines of suffering have found a place
Already there too early. His swift glance,
Sharp and unflinching, makes us ask the earth
Why on her rack a sensitive soul is grilled
With grueling pain, and why such promising worth
Is snatched back to her bosom unfulfilled.
Is there an answer? Ah! I sometimes think
He saw too plain the spirit of the world,
And found it evil, saw it on the brink
Of its supreme disaster, hates unfurled
Of nation bombing nation, saw afar
And said, "There never will be an end of war."

XII

When I remember lovers on the green
Fair page of history, I straightway recall
How great a lover Stephen might have been
And pine with grief that he should miss it all.
His thought for others in the little things
That make a household rich, the patient care
He lavished on his Christmas offerings
Revealed what boundless love was his to share.
The faithfulness that others know in part
Was his in ample fullness, all the ways
He opened up the greatness of his heart
Were milestones in the measure of our days.
Such love as his no scholarship can gauge;
But O how fair the script on his brief page!

XIII

A call comes for the clothing he will wear
On his last journey into mother earth,
The hardest of all offices to bear
Is here—for even his socks proclaim the mirth
And gaiety that marked his schoolboy taste,
The shirt and tie as colored as the coat

274

That Joseph wore upon the Midian waste—
And death's contingency O so remote!
The clothes are ironed lovingly—each press
Sealed by a mother's memories and tears,
As mothers through all time have borne the stress,
And lived by some endurance that appears
Granted by unseen powers from a source
That quite transcends man's natural recourse.

XIV

'Tis not the painful loss to us we feel
Most deeply in his passing, though that stroke
Outweighs all other strains that sorrow's yoke
Has put upon us; 'tis for his own weal
We mourn; his days of youth cut off, the peal
Of friendly singing in a college hall,
The joys of wife and children, and the call
Of ocean, mountain, lake with rod and reel.
But most of all we mourn what earth has lost—
Integrity that happens here below
Too seldom for her good—he dared her frost,
And felt her blight and her Antarctic snow,
Uncompromising as a Joan of Arc,
He trusted earth and found her shadows dark.

XV

The empty plate upon the Christmas table,
The empty stocking and the vacant chair,
How on this Christmastide shall we be able
To brave the children's voices on the stair?
'Twas dark when each one rushed to find his stocking,
But O how darker now with him away!
How we shall miss the shouts and eager talking
That changed our late December into May!
We were the wise ones coming from the East,
We were the shepherds hearing, in the blue,
Angelic singing for the world's great feast—
The star that led them to their rendezvous.
Now in the face of our bereaving pain,
We know how Herod's edict left its stain.

XVI

How shall we face the sea with him away,
With him away who held the main stroke oar
To steady us through channel, strait, and bay,
And find us anchorage on a harbored shore?
He entered with bold eagerness for sailing
Upon the voyage of his few brief years;
And when reverses came, and we were railing
'Twas his calm spirit that resolved our fears.
We sail without him now, but not without
The legacy of fortitude he gave,
The legacy of humor that held out
Through every gale of suffering. O brave
And precious spirit, still remain our guide
Till we, like you, have shuffled earth aside.

XVII

Did we love earth too much? I ask, or may
Some medieval schoolman ask through me?
Take life too much as one long holiday
In northern woods, the Rockies, and the sea?
We sailed among the islands, fished and camped
The country over like a gipsy brood
That knows the strength of out-of-doors; we champed
At the bit when bridles held us too subdued.
And is this stroke, this breaking of the chain,
A grim reminder that our sojourn here
Is but a bivouac in the long campaign
Of man's unending tilt with faith and fear,
Fear of the dark, and faith that sees the Light
Chasing the shadows of earth's temporal night?

Glossary of Maine Coast Words

Banshee, a ghost that appears in the shape of an animal to warn one of his death. Irish.

Barvel, an oilcloth garment worn on the lower part of the body when hauling traps. It is shaped like a woman's skirt.

Bolin, a knot.

Butty, stoneworkers' word for mate or "buddy."

Count lobster, a lobster of the prescribed legal length.

Ditty box, a sailor's small box which holds thread, needles, tape, letters, etc.

Fore-and-after, a vessel whose sails are not supported by yards, but carried on gaffs and booms.

Ghunk hole, an onomatopoeia. An imitation of the sound of rough waves under headland cliffs.

Grout bank, a pile of chipped-off stone.

Gurry, the scum and slime that collects on lobster pots or warps or on the skin of fish.

Honey pots, quicksand formations in mud coves.

Hooker, same as *fore-and-after.*

Keening, weeping in sympathy with one who has met with a loss. Irish.

Killock, an anchor for a small boat, made by fastening a rock between a couple of spruce or other boughs.

Lumber-johnny, a lumber-carrying coasting vessel from the English provinces, usually from Canada. She almost invariably has no bowsprit.

Moithered, disturbed or bothered. Irish.

Morphodite, a corrupt Maine coast pronunciation for "hermaphrodite."

Paving motion, paving quarry. On the Maine coast, "quarry" is reserved as the name of the place from which the larger stone is excavated.

Plug-drill, to drill short holes in stone in a row for the purpose of breaking it.

Pocket, pound, and *leader.* The three parts of a herring weir.

Popple stones, beach pebbles washed smooth by the waves. An almost exact Anglo-Saxon survival still in use on the coast.

Quawk, the qua bird or night heron, named for the sound it makes.

Reel blocks, to, to trim the rough edges off the paving blocks.

Room of, instead of.

Soggarth, an Irish word for priest.

Spider, a New England word for frying pan.

Square-rigger, a vessel whose principal sails are extended on yards suspended horizontally at the middle.

Thraneen, what is left over after the table is cleared. Irish.

Toggle, a small buoy, part way between the main buoy and the trap, used to keep the rope from catching on the bottom of the bay.

Tollers, decoys.

Touse, disturbance.

Warp, the rope attached to a lobster pot.

White ash breeze, a metaphor used on the coast to indicate propelling a boat by oars instead of by sail.

Whisht, keep still. Irish.

Windjammer, same as *fore-and-after.*

The Collected Poems of Wilbert Snow
was composed in Linotype Caledonia and printed
by offset lithography by Wesleyan University
Press Incorporated. The binding was done by
Vail-Ballou Press, Inc. The drawings were made
for this edition by Raymond M. Grimaila.

Wesleyan University Press
MIDDLETOWN, CONNECTICUT

ST. MARY'S COLLEGE OF MARYLAND
ST. MARY'S CITY, MARYLAND

40996